Get Your GOLF On!

Your Guide to
Getting in the Game

by Debbie Waitkus

GOLF FOR CAUSE

Get Your Golf On!

Photography by Jim Amrine

Cover design and interior layout by Brandi Hollister, Mullins Creative
www.mullinscreative.com

Published by
Golf for Cause®, LLC
570 W. Southern Ave., Tempe, AZ 85282
www.golfforcause.com

ISBN # 978-0-9858220-0-2

Acknowledgements

Get Your Golf On! started as an idea. An idea that I placed on a tee and, like some things in life, it stayed on that tee until I finally stepped up and took a swing, sending it into play. With much joy and appreciation, that idea is now in your hands! I had a lot of encouragement and support along the way… from tee to green.

Joining me on the tee, I'm thankful to all the Nine & Winers – with special thanks to the amazing mentors, particularly Char Carson, whose passion and commitment to growing others through golf always shines, Kevin & Cindy Sonoda, Brian Davis (when are you coming back to Phoenix?), Karen Maish (do you bribe all your groups to say you're the best?!), Curt Clark, Ellen Friese and the open-minded Golf Academy of America students. And the teeing grounds are always best at Starfire Golf Club, Silverado Golf Course, Mountain Shadows Golf Course and Continental Golf Course, where the staff is warm, open minded and committed to growing new golfers. Laura Martini, thanks for inviting me to play and insisting that we'd have fun! And to Bower Yousse, Maurine Karabatsos and my MM ladies - Silver Rose, Joyce (Rosie) Friel, Kay McDonald, Susan Brooks and Vickie McDermott, thank you for your strong presence on the tee!

Advancing *Get Your Golf On!* down the fairway, thank-you Jake Poiner for helping me keep my ball in play! High fives to some of the best playing partners around: My colleagues in the National Women's Golf Alliance: Debbie O'Connell and Lynn Stellman with Ladies Links Fore Golf, Jan Bel Jan with Jan Bel Jan Golf Course Design and Pam Swensen with the Executive Women's Golf Association; Pam Wright, LPGA; Kathy Murphy, LPGA; Essay Vanderbilt (Dr. V) and Gerri Jordan with Yar Golf; Karen Lovcik with Glove It; Taba Dale with The Scottsdale Collection; Deborah Bateman with National Bank of Arizona; Jeff Sorkness and Mike Friend with Troon Golf; Steve Collins with Pirnaha Golf; Peggy Gustafson, LPGA; Sue Wieger, LPGA; my colleagues in Women in the Golf Industry (WIGI) – special shout outs to Kathy Bissell with Coldwell Banker, Barb Hanson with

Corporate Golf Services, Rosemary Johnson with the Ladies Golf Journey, Danelle Kelling with Stinson Morrison Hecker, Emmy Moore with Moore Minister Consulting Group, Pat Mullaly with GolfGurls.com, Elizabeth Noblitt with ShiShi Putter, Katherine Roberts with Yoga for Golfers and Christina Thompson with Golf4Her. And to the TTFNers, way to keep golf (and life) fun – always! Larry Wilk needs special mention for teaching me the finer points of golf – like matching beverage selections to my wardrobe, and Lana Hock for the importance of a great golf wardrobe… especially the hats!

Marilynn Smith, I love your trailblazing spirit, can-do attitude and voice in my head reminding me to "hold my finish" – a great reminder to follow through on everything I do.

Thanks to my children who know that golf is fun! Ben – always ready with a bet for shots over the water. Amy, who dribbled the ball off the tee at her first Nine & Wine outing and decided that she'd just ride in the cart for the day, was inspired to play and proclaimed golf as being "fun" after she watched one of her playing partners tee up a ball in the fairway for her second shot.

Clearly my favorite playing partners in the entire world are my husband, Jack Waitkus and my mom Lois (who learned to play golf in her 60s when she married Maury, a passionate four-time-a-week golfer – thanks, Maury!). She read the manuscript and proclaimed it the Bible! Without their help *Get Your Golf On!* would never have made it to the green.

Vickie Mullins and Ted Rogers with Perfect Bound Marketing, thank you for tending the flag on my final hole, helping me sink the putt! Hats off to photographer extraordinaire, Jim Amrine, now, the newest golfer to be seen at the driving range – in spite of the Arizona summer heat and his two artificial hips!

And to my caddie – Bower Yousse, my permanent guest at the 19th hole, thank you for carrying my bag and helping me find my voice. Without your collaboration, *Get Your Golf On!* would still be sitting on the tee.

Table of Contents

Foreword

When I was 11, I was the pitcher, coach and manager of a boys baseball team in my hometown of Topeka, Kansas — and thought nothing of being the only one sporting pigtails under my cap. I had my sights set on being a pitcher for the St. Louis Cardinals baseball team.

One day I came home after pitching a game and my mom asked, "How did it go today, dear?" I threw my glove across the room and said a few choice words that landed me in the bathroom, getting my mouth washed out with soap.

With the taste of Lifebuoy still fresh on my tongue, I dreaded what was headed my way when my dad got home. But, instead, he said something that would change my life: "We'd better take her out to the Wichita Country Club and teach her a more ladylike sport." The fact was, however, girls in the '40s weren't even supposed to play golf — we were supposed to get married and raise families.

That rang true when I went to the University of Kansas, which didn't have a golf team for girls at the time. Moreover, when my dad asked legendary basketball coach Phog Allen (who was the University's athletic director at the time) if there might be some expense money so I could play in the National Intercollegiate Championship at Ohio State, he responded, "Mr. Smith, it's too bad your daughter isn't a boy."

 Looking back, despite some bumps along the way, things turned out better than a freckled, pigtailed girl from Kansas ever could have hoped. Golf gave me an opportunity to excel at a sport and therefore to pursue a dream. I've always felt that God put me in the right place at the right time. A baker's dozen of us founded the LPGA in 1950, drumming up support for the tour as well as playing on it. I cherish every tournament memory with my friends — the 21 victories, two major championships, and induction into the World Golf Hall of Fame were simply delicious icing on an incredible cake.

Thanks to golf, I've had the opportunity to make friends in all 50 states and in 37 countries around the world, broadening my horizons in ways that I have to pinch myself to believe. I've performed exhibitions at air bases in France and Germany, and I've been fortunate enough to meet five U.S. Presidents. And, for the past 11 years, golf has enabled me to pay it forward with charity tournaments to support the Marilynn Smith Scholarship Fund, which helps young girls fund their college experiences.

Golf is a humbling game, and it teaches you something new every time you step up to the tee. It reveals your own character — and the character of those around you. But, more than anything, it underscores the amazing things that happen when you enjoy what you're doing and grow with the results.

That, for me, is at the heart of this book. I met Debbie Waitkus when she played in the Marilynn Smith LPGA Championship in 2009. Unbeknownst to me, she was in the audience at my induction ceremony to the World Golf Hall of Fame and subsequently wrote a story about me, which was published. We became fast friends after the 2009 tournament, and her efforts, energy, and talent as the co-tournament director made it possible for nine young ladies to each earn a $5,000 scholarship in 2010, and in 2011, ten were each awarded a $10,000 scholarship. She's a jewel.

I think you'll find that Debbie's approach to introducing beginners to this wonderful game is a drive straight down the middle.

Marilynn Smith
LPGA Co-Founder
World Golf Hall of Fame Inductee (2006)
Winner of 21 LPGA tournaments including 2 majors
Inaugural Patty Berg Award Recipient (1978)
Created and promoted the first Senior LPGA tournament (2001)
LPGA president (1958-1960)
Started LPGA TC&P (Teaching & Club Professional)
  with Shirley Spork (1959)
Conducted over 4,000 golf clinics

Prelude To Your Adventure...

Pam Wright

Anyone who plays golf understands how challenging it can be. But, as a result of the game's challenges, players gain an inherent respect for each other — particularly those who play the game as it was intended. By joining the game, you are also joining an extended social family with its own peculiar rules and traditions and a cast of fun, interesting, and occasionally quirky characters.

As a reader of this book, you're undoubtedly coming to the sport from a bit of a different angle than my own. My dad was a golf pro in my native Scotland, and my mom played at a very high level in her own right. I first picked up a club at age four, earned a college scholarship to Arizona State University, and enjoyed a 15-year career on the LPGA Tour.

In the years since retiring from professional golf, I've had the good fortune to stay in the game as a teaching professional. About a third of my clients are beginners, though the overall talent pool runs the gamut — and, believe me, just because someone has played for 30 years doesn't mean they can break 100.

I've found that, for many new to the game, the biggest hurdle is the process of becoming comfortable — or, as many of my students have expressed it, overcoming the anxiety of "I don't know if I can do that." That's exactly what this book is all about — preparing to experience the game, whether you're one of those people who will just barrel in and have a go at it or one who's on the more tentative side.

I believe a new golfer's greatest asset is often enthusiasm. It's always invigorating to have someone on the lesson tee who's "into it," regardless of the specific motivation for learning to play. When that person heads out on the course, it can even rekindle the spark for more experienced and serious players who long ago forgot the thrill of their first good shots. They just have to stop and say, "Wow, she's having a blast!"

As an adult beginner, after all, you're in a bit of unique position —
you're starting out as someone who's *choosing* to venture out onto
the tees, fairways and greens. My best advice is to surround yourself
with people who make it enjoyable. Go with some friends, hit some
shots, get some help from an instructor, and see where it takes you.

Golf's a game. Keep it fun!

Pam Wright
Pam Wright Golf
www.pamwrightgolf.com

1989 LPGA Rookie of the Year
1990, 1992, 1994 Solheim Cup Competitor
2000, 2002 Solheim Cup Vice Captain
22 Top 10 finishes on LPGA Tour
Recorded lowest 9-hole score of 30 in US Open history
Arizona State University Hall of Fame
Two-time Pac-10 Champion
Academic All-American
Two Time All-American
1979 - 1987 Scottish Internationalist

Introduction

When I was pregnant, I had on my nightstand a copy of *What to Expect When You're Expecting.*

It was a popular book with moms-to-be because it prepared us for what was to come and provided reassurance we'd survive the experience just fine. I soon learned no book can prepare a person 100% for delivery day and diapers, but I found it helpful in understanding the scope of what I'd gotten myself into. It was the memory of that book that inspired this book.

I can report that nine months of pregnancy and taking up the game of golf aren't that much alike, but over the years, I've encountered many newcomers who arrive at my golf clinics and outings with delivery-room nervousness. The majority of them are women.

I admit that setting out to become a golfer can be an intimidating experience, especially if you don't have a clue where to begin. It is, for almost everyone. It was for me.

My goal for *Get Your Golf On!* is to remove the intimidation factor so that for you, starting out can be easy and will always be fun. This isn't an instruction book on how to hit a golf ball, however. You learn to do *that* hitting golf balls and taking lessons, although taking lessons is not mandatory. (Does the name Bubba Watson, 2012 Masters Champion, ring a bell? Never had a lesson.) Nonetheless, your local teaching professional can help you advance your game.

Get Your Golf On! draws on my experience and the experiences of thousands of beginner golfers who have participated in my *Nine &*

Wine (www.nineandwine.com) golf outings. At *Nine & Wine* we have fun learning to look, act, think, talk, and laugh like golfers. We even play nine holes! Our objective is to demystify golf so completely that, when you leave, you can go to any golf course and feel confident and comfortable.

So let's get your golf on and begin the wonderful experience that will enrich your life in countless ways.

~ Debbie Waitkus

Gayle Moss
Marketing Consultant
www.on-mark-it.com

"It took me 45 years to discover my love for golf, but once I experienced the joys of playing the game and challenging myself to get better, I've never looked back. For me, golf is much more than 'a game for life;' golf IS my life.

"My father and brother were avid golfers, but in my youth, boys golfed and girls figure skated. When I moved to Vancouver, BC in 2003 I saw that people enjoyed golf here year round – a rare thing in Canada. I was dating a man at the time who hadn't golfed in years, but wanted to take it up again. So after decades of playing spectator, I decided to give it a try in 2004.

"After some excellent instruction and a few 'come back tomorrow' shots, I've become addicted to all things golf and started writing about it – first on my golfgal.ca blog, then on Golf for Women Magazine's website and now for InsideGolf.ca. When I'm not golfing or writing about it, I am an independent marketing consultant. I am often asked by clients to play golf with them and their customers, which helps grow my network and business opportunities.

"On the personal side, I am now married to that man who encouraged me to take up the sport in 2004. He loves the game almost as much as I do and is my first choice in a playing partner. Golf gave us a dream and we're living it!"

Chapter 1

Little Did I Know

"Don't fear failure so much that you refuse to try new things. The saddest summary of a life contains three descriptions: could have, might have, and should have."

~ Louis E. Boone

When you are learning something new, it's important to trust the person teaching you. You have to believe your teacher has credibility, that she knows what she is talking about. To establish my street — er, grass — cred, here is the story of my first golf experience. (If you think *you* don't know enough about golf, listen to this!)

I didn't discover golf on my own. I discovered golf only after a friend dragged me into it.

Laura was a colleague whose uncle had recently begun teaching her to play. Almost overnight she had become an enthusiast, a fanatic actually, and she was determined to get me involved too. "Come on, Debbie," she pleaded. "Just give it a try. I know you'll love it!"

I knew I wouldn't love it. I'd grown up playing every sport a girl could play, except golf. Golf didn't interest me. It sounded boring. But my arm was starting to hurt from Laura twisting it, so I gave in. "One time," I said, "and that's all."

I was nervous about a few things and feared that Laura, in her zeal, had overlooked some important issues. I didn't have any golf clubs. Nor golf shoes. Nor proper golf attire. It was summer — in Phoenix, Arizona — which meant we'd be playing in triple-digit heat. I have an artificial knee as the result of a serious soccer injury in college. Oh, and I was pregnant. And do they have bathrooms at the golf course? *A lot* of bathrooms?

Although I was tempted to bail out, I called my mom and asked whether she had any golf clubs in her garage. She called back moments later. "They're dusty. And you'll still need a **Driver.**" This news gave me a boost, because it seemed things were starting to go my way — I didn't need a Driver; Laura said we'd be using **pull carts**. I just needed comfortable shoes. It didn't occur to me that a Driver is a golf club.

Finding something to wear wasn't the problem I expected it to be. I had only to dress respectfully. We weren't going to a fashion show, for goodness sake. Shorts with pockets for my tissues? *Check.* Collared shirt light enough to be comfortable in the heat — and big enough to cover a pregnant woman's belly? *Looking... in husband's closet... check.*

On game day I arrived at downtown Phoenix's 9-hole Encanto **Executive Course** right on time. Or so I thought. In the **clubhouse**, as I paid my **green fee**, the cashier instructed me to hurry to join my group on the **first tee**. *Group?*

I ran, clubs rattling in the pull cart behind me. I was all arms and legs and belly. And high-top sneakers. And my husband's billowing polo shirt. My group — Laura and three male co-workers — watched my approach, awed. I had no idea, of course, that I was a fifth wheel! Golf is typically played in foursomes.

That day, I learned that golfers enjoy introducing the game to newcomers and making it a fun experience. They delight in teaching you the language of golf and use gentle humor to put you at ease.

My first shot went 30 yards and disappeared into a thicket of oleander. *(I made contact! Woo-hoo!)* Big Phil from Atlanta, a country boy with the sweetest southern drawl I'd ever heard, followed me to the thicket to help look for my ball.

"Do y'all have a foot wedge in your bag, Miss Debbie?" he asked. I was sure I did because, according to my mother, all I was missing was a Driver. I searched through the clubs in vain. I found numbered clubs, an "SW" and a "PW," but no "FW." I looked up in dismay. Big Phil grinned and kicked my ball into the **fairway**. "There ya go, Miss Debbie. That's a foot wedge."

Twenty years have passed since that day. I still recall everything about it. How beautiful the course was with all its green grass fairways, palm trees and flowering oleanders! How amazing it was to be hitting golf balls in a setting surrounded by the city. How profoundly it enhanced my already good working relationships with three male colleagues whose superior I was at the office! Most of all, I recall how much *fun* it was. Laura was right. I did love it.

In 2000 I left my position as president of a firm in the corporate financial world to create *Golf for Cause*®, a company that focuses on helping organizations and individuals use golf as a tool to raise money, build relationships and promote personal growth. Thousands of golfers, many of them women and a large percentage of them beginners, have participated in our various workshops, conferences, clinics, tournaments and just-for-fun events to learn how to *turn golf into gold*®.

Maurine Karabatsos
Director of Strategic Alliance
Empire West Title Agency

"For me it was necessity. I think many women golfers get started out of necessity. I was working in a mostly male, certainly male-dominated banking environment. My title and responsibilities were the same as the men in the office, but I wasn't 'one of the guys.' The guys would come back to the office after a round of golf and they'd be talking about things I hadn't been privy to. Things I needed to know. I realized that they weren't just playing golf — they were doing business, too. I needed to get in the game.

"When I left the banking industry to start a new career in the title business, people kept calling me with questions about banking, which I was glad to answer, but it wasn't helping me in the title industry. One day it occurred to me to get the banking people together with the title people. Even though it was summer, and hot, golf seemed like the way to do it. I've been doing business on the golf course ever since."

Debbie Hill
Attorney and Consultant
President, La Cerra Sueno LLC

"No matter what business you are in, getting new work is all about new relationships. In a previous career I was a criminal defense lawyer. My playing partners were not likely to need my services the next day, but they could pass my name along. And they did. The game of golf is an ideal networking tool because it reaches into so many areas of interest and offers something for everyone."

Chapter 2

You Can
Say That Again!

*"One can never consent to creep
when one feels an impulse to soar."*

~ Helen Keller

You hear the funniest things on a golf course. Some words and expressions don't seem to make sense, because they mean one thing on the course and something entirely different in everyday usage. Golf language can be quite colorful, too, and jargon varies from geographical region to geographical region. Making up new words is always encouraged and can create wonderful memories.

Golf has its share of four-letter words, even an "F" word. That word is **"FORE!"** You shout this word as loud as you can when you hit a shot that looks as if it may hit another golfer. There's an "S" word, too — our "S" word is "special," and it means the same thing that other "S" word does. Ours is just a nicer way of saying it.

I'm not encouraging profanity here. Tension can be very destructive to your attitude and your swing. When you hit one of those wayward shots, keep an eye on where it goes and simply declare, "Wasn't that special." Not only will you find some humor in it and put the rest of your foursome at ease, you'll help yourself let go of any negativity. Try it! I suspect you'll say the "S" word with a smile!

You've already noticed that some words in this book are in **bold**. These words and others are in the golf lingo glossary at the back of the book. Check it out for a listing of golf's descriptive and often clever terminology. Most of them are self-explanatory, although you may have to think about them for a moment. A few are part of golf's lexicon despite making no sense to anyone. **Duck hook**, for example, describes a right-handed golfer's shot when it curves sharply right to left and stays low to the ground. "Hook" is understandable. "Duck," not so much. But you'll hear it.

Golfers talk less to each other than they talk to themselves, their golf balls, the sky, God, and even invisible people. But it is all in fun and there is actually a good reason for it: you release the frustration that sometimes comes when you hit a ball that doesn't go where you hoped it would.

Margaret Dunn
Owner
Atypical Transportation Company
Dunn Transportation Company

"My ex and I used to go out and hack around at a golf course, and I'd play when asked, but it was always just about being outdoors and having a beer. After my divorce I started playing with my sister and brother-in-law at a course near their time-share in Arizona, because I thought it might be a nice way to meet men. Of course I didn't want to embarrass myself, so I took six lessons from the pro. Now I am the instigator of playing golf!

"I created Dunn Transportation to get more involved in the business of golf. Our executive coaches are designed to transport as many as 36 passengers, or 6 foursomes and their golf bags — bags are kept upright, mind you. But I play golf to have fun and laugh my $%#&! off. It's a great way to meet people and a great way to break the ice. Mention that you play golf and a conversation starts."

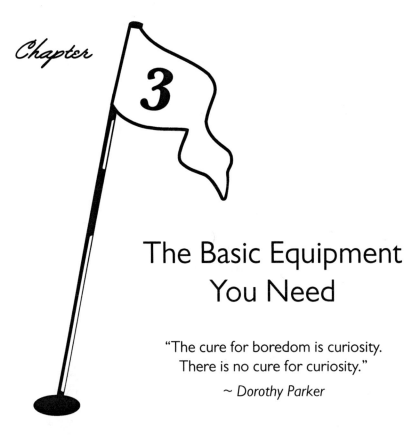

3

The Basic Equipment You Need

*"The cure for boredom is curiosity.
There is no cure for curiosity."*

~ Dorothy Parker

To play golf, you need equipment, same as any other sport. Baseball, you need a bat and a ball. Tennis, a racket and a ball. Golf, clubs and a ball. *Clubs? More than one?* Yes. In golf, you need a variety of clubs to obtain a variety of results. The way the ball flies through the air when you hit it depends on which club you use. This is one of the reasons hitting golf balls can be so much fun.

Golf Clubs

Some golf newcomers find "the whole golf club thing" confusing. So let's begin with a few simple observations:

- Every player must have a golf bag with golf clubs in it.
- The golf bag can have up to 14 clubs, but no more.
- Beginning golfers typically don't need all 14 clubs.

- There are clubs for left-hand golfers and clubs for righties.
- There are clubs for women and clubs for men (although some women prefer to play with men's clubs).

A typical full set of women's clubs generally consists of:

- 1-Wood (Driver)
- 3-Wood (also called a Fairway Metal)
- 5-Wood (also called a Fairway Metal)
- 7-Wood (also called a Fairway Metal)
- Two Hybrid clubs (also called Rescue Clubs)
- 6-Iron
- 7-Iron
- 8-Iron
- 9-Iron
- Pitching Wedge
- Sand Wedge
- Putter

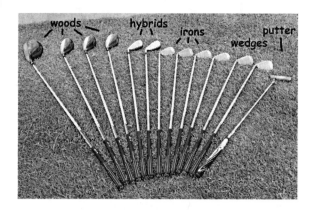

Some golf club manufacturers offer a "partial" or "basic" set of clubs, which contains fewer clubs than a full set. This might be an attractive option for you as a new golfer. The partial set might include a Driver, 3-wood, hybrid club, 7-iron, 9-iron, Sand Wedge and even a golf bag!

NOTE: A typical full set of men's clubs has a slightly different composition: instead of two hybrid clubs, the men's set might have a 3-iron, a 4-iron and an additional wedge.

So many clubs, so many choices! Why?

Different clubs send the golf ball different distances and give it different trajectories. Here's an easy way to understand the numbers on the clubs: the higher the number, the higher the ball trajectory and the shorter the distance the ball goes. (And also the shorter distance it rolls after it lands.) Another way to look at it is this: picture a child playing with a garden hose, trying to soak someone nearby. Raising the hose to make the water go higher SHORTENS the distance it travels. Also, the water hits the ground with a splat and doesn't get much farther. The same principle applies to your golf clubs: use a higher number club and the result is a higher, shorter shot.

Today, many golf club manufacturers print the degree of loft on each club, which makes it even easier to determine which club you want to use. A sand wedge, for example, is 56°, so the ball should go high, but not far. A Driver, at 12°, will make the ball fly lower and much farther than the sand wedge.

You are allowed to carry any combination of clubs you desire, up to 14 clubs, in your golf bag. Although these combinations are impractical, you could choose to carry only two Drivers and nothing else, or four wedges, or 14 putters — any combination.

Very often, new golfers start out with golf clubs borrowed from a friend or relative. This is a perfectly acceptable, financially sound decision, but a strong word of caution:

> Men's golf clubs are heavier than women's clubs. They typically have stiffer, steel shafts rather than lighter-weight graphite shafts, and the shafts may be longer. All of this works to a woman's disadvantage, is detrimental to performance and enjoyment, and can be exhausting, as well. If you are a woman and borrow clubs, try to borrow a woman's set.

> Also, when you borrow clubs, it is likely that they are someone's old or second set. Beggars can't be choosers, but golf club manufacturing technology continues to improve club quality and performance, so much so that clubs only a few years old won't help you play your best.

Borrowing or renting clubs allows you to get a feel for the game before you incur the expense of purchasing your own clubs. When you do decide to buy clubs, I strongly encourage you to buy them from a store or golf facility that will "fit" you to your clubs.

You'll read more about golf clubs in Chapter 5, *Let's Go To The Driving Range.*

Golf Bag

You need a golf bag in which to carry your clubs. There are many styles and brands of bags to choose from. Some bags are designed for golfers who prefer to walk when they play, as opposed to riding in a golf cart. These bags are lighter weight, have retractable "stand up" legs, and are usually smaller than "cart" bags, which are the choice of golfers who prefer riding to walking.

Every golf bag has pockets, and you may discover that the number of pockets is one of your most important considerations. You'll need a pocket for your golf balls, certainly, but you'll also want pockets for your golf tees, pencils, sunscreen, snacks, car keys, business cards, and perhaps even a water bottle.

Be sure to put your name on your golf bag. A luggage tag works great, or you can purchase one of the tags available at golf stores and pro shops.

NOTE: *Two additional items to have with your golf bag are a ball retriever (a retractable tool to retrieve your ball from water when you make one of those "special" shots) and a golf towel for cleaning your clubs. Clean clubs perform better.*

Golf Balls

As a new golfer, choosing the kind of golf balls you want to play may seem confusing when you see how many there are to choose from. It can be even more confusing if you read the blurbs on the boxes. So don't do that. My advice to beginners is this: simply start with the least expensive balls. The kind of ball you play will only be a concern once your skill level improves significantly.

Some balls are marked "Ladies," but this has more to do with marketing than performance characteristics. If you look closely you will even see a particular brand of balls called "Laddies." *Precept,* the manufacturer, discovered that quite a few men were playing *Precept* "Ladies" balls because they went farther, yet the men felt a bit awkward about it. It was an easy problem to solve: the manufacturer changed the "Ladies" to "Laddies" and promoted the "new" ball.

You'll also notice that golf balls are available in colors other than white. If you like pink, great. Orange or yellow or lime green? Great. Whatever you like is fine.

NOTE: *If you are concerned about the environment, Dixon Golf (DixonGolf.com) manufactures a line of balls that are 100% recyclable. And they even sell a ladies golf ball, the "Dixon Spirit." They also have a recycling program that allows you to exchange old balls for new ones at a discount.*

How many golf balls should you carry in your bag? Most golfers carry a dozen, plus or minus a few.

Stephanie McCoy Loquvam
Attorney At Law

"I had always heard about business getting done on the golf course, and I had considered that I should take up golf, but I was always in school. The law firm I joined was exactly what I was looking for. The only catch was that I would be the only female lawyer. This did not bother me in the least. My first attorney retreat was about 5 weeks after I started with the firm. I received an agenda for the weekend, planned by our female administrator, and glanced over the activities — group functions, dinners with spouses and spa appointments. I looked at my husband's itinerary and saw some of the same group functions, the dinner and *golf*.

"After distributing the itineraries, the administrator approached me and said she had booked a tee time for my husband with the men and an appointment for me at the spa with the wives. She asked if this was okay and suggested she could change it if necessary. I agreed to keep my spa appointment to make things easy — but I was committed that never again would I be in the spa group."

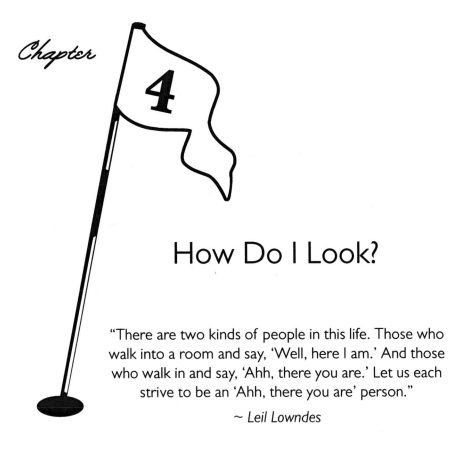

How Do I Look?

"There are two kinds of people in this life. Those who walk into a room and say, 'Well, here I am.' And those who walk in and say, 'Ahh, there you are.' Let us each strive to be an 'Ahh, there you are' person."

~ *Leil Lowndes*

If you love clothes and fashion, you will love shopping for golf attire. Golf clothing is designed for fashion and function. But it isn't a rule that you have to wear clothes specifically designed for golf. Wardrobe rules are very simple, in fact:

- Almost all golf courses require collared shirts for men.
- Women's shirts, if sleeveless, must have a collar; if the shirt has sleeves, no collar is necessary.
- Shorts are fine, but not short shorts.
- Denim anything is a no-no.
- Sneakers are okay if you don't have golf shoes.

Shorts, skorts, capris and slacks should have pockets large enough to put your hand into. The first time I played golf I chose to wear shorts with pockets because I needed a place to put my tissues. I didn't realize I'd need pockets for other things — an extra ball, a few **tees**, a **ball marker**, and a **divot repair tool**.

Have fun with your wardrobe. Just remember that you'll be bending over a lot, squatting, twisting your body and raising your arms.

Hats, Caps And Visors

Yes! Always bring something to protect your head from the elements.

Golf Glove

Most golfers prefer to wear a glove because they feel it helps them grip the club. You may prefer to not wear a glove. But keep this is mind:

- A right-handed golfer wears the glove on her LEFT hand.
- A left-handed golfer wears the glove on her RIGHT hand.

Wearing the glove on the "wrong" hand will make sense to you when you start hitting balls.

Note that some golf gloves have a ball marker that you can use on the green integrated right into their design.

Golf Shoes

When you buy golf shoes, be sure they are very comfortable — you'll be doing a lot of walking. There are many great styles and colors to choose from, but comfort is your most important consideration.

Most golf shoes have removable soft spikes (virtually all golf courses no longer allow the old-fashioned steel spikes), but not all spikes fit all shoes. When your spikes get worn down and need to be replaced, bring one of the spikes or one of your shoes to the store to be sure you get the right type. Also, it is a good idea to check the tightness of spikes on new shoes — sometimes the factory ships them untightened. (It takes a special tool to tighten them, but if you don't have one, the golf shops will always assist you.)

You'll also see some golf shoes that are spikeless, sporting nubs on their bottoms that do not need to be replaced. They're quite comfortable and very acceptable to wear on the golf course.

NOTE: New shoes may cause blisters Be prepared: keep a few Band-Aids® or moleskin in your golf bag. If you need a Band-Aid and don't have one, ask in the pro shop — they can almost always help you.

Wardrobe Extras

Depending on the weather, you may want to put a windbreaker or sweater in your bag. A golf umbrella can also come in handy, so if it looks like rain is a possibility, take one. Most golf bags have a special umbrella holder on the outside of the bag.

Deborah Bateman
Executive Vice President, Wealth Strategies
National Bank of Arizona

"Part of my job is creating and developing new relationships, and I've found the perfect vehicle for it. A golf cart. Once a month a private banker colleague and I organize a golf outing using my 'Women Who Golf' list, which is a collection of names of professional women who answered affirmatively when I asked, 'Do you play golf?' We assemble two foursomes of women who may or may not know each other but have golf in common. Four and a half hours on the golf course, followed by a drink afterward, is a great way to start a relationship. We all talk about what we do and almost always discover opportunities to work together or help one another. You'd be surprised how many women make the financial decisions in the household. The reason I know this is because a lot of men come to my office and say, 'My wife told me to come talk to you.' Sure enough, she was in one of our foursomes. Is golf a good marketing tool? Unquestionably."

Let's Go To The Driving Range

"Don't be afraid to look unfeminine by taking a whole-hearted whack with the club. Anyone strong enough to lift a two-year-old child or tote a vacuum cleaner or a bag of groceries can hit a powerful shot."

~ Sharron Moran

You have clubs. You look like a golfer. Now you need to hit some balls to get comfortable with your clubs — keeping in mind the old saying, "Practice makes perfect." So let's go to the driving range!

Most golf courses have driving ranges or practice areas that are separate from the golf course. This means that you can pay for a bucket of practice balls without having to pay a green fee as you would for an actual game.

Most cities have driving ranges that are not connected to a golf course. These practice facilities often have lights for nighttime practice — a nice way to spend an hour after work or later in the evening! Also, driving ranges are great places to meet people and make new friends.

Here are a few things to think about before you get to the driving range:

The driving range is a place to have fun in a casual setting while you are getting familiar with your golf clubs — figuring out how you grip them; how you position yourself to hit the ball (how you "address" it); how you swing; and how far the ball goes depending on which club you use.

After you purchase a small or large bucket (or basket or bag) of balls (usually from $5 - $12 per bucket), take the bucket and your golf clubs to the practice area where other golfers are practicing. You may want to take only a few clubs with you rather than your whole bag.

A note about purchasing practice balls: depending on where you go, you may be handed a bucket of balls, or you may be given a receipt to show the outside attendant or a token to put in a machine that will spit out a bucket of balls. The balls may already be at the hitting area. In any case, keep your receipt handy, as you may have to show it to someone. If you have to get the balls from a machine, BE SURE TO PUT THE BUCKET UNDER THE DISPENSER FIRST. If you forget to do this, 50 -100 golf balls will spill out and go all over the place. And it wouldn't be the first time *that's* happened!

Before you start hitting balls, always be sure to do a few minutes of stretching exercises to loosen your body and warm up your muscles. This is very important at the driving range because, here, you are hitting balls at a much faster pace than when you are playing golf on a course.

While you are warming up, observe the other golfers. Quite often the people hitting balls are accomplished golfers, so you can learn by watching them. Note how they grip their clubs, bend their knees, position their feet, hold their heads, and swing. When you see a golfer hitting nice shot after nice shot, that's a good golfer to watch. If you feel awkward studying someone's form and swing, ask if he or she is okay with it.

*M*ost golfers prefer practicing on real grass, but some practice facilities may ask at times that you to hit off synthetic turf mats. This won't hurt you, but it doesn't feel quite right because it isn't what you experience on real grass. Also, you may find a small rubber tube sticking up on the left or right side of the synthetic mats. This acts as a tee.

Which Club To Hit First?

Start with a wedge. It is the shortest of your clubs and will give you an opportunity to ease into your swings. Take note of the colored flags in the landing area in front of you. Choose one as your target and try to hit toward it consistently.

Always watch where your ball lands, because you are on an important mission: by trying out your different clubs, you are seeking to identify which one is your "100-yard club." Be patient with yourself, because your swing is not yet repeating (meaning that it's not yet the same, swing after swing after swing). You may have to go to the practice range several times before you can determine which club is your 100-yard club.

Your 100-Yard Club: The Key To The Kingdom — Er, Queendom

Once you have determined which of your clubs makes the ball go approximately 100 yards, you've made a HUGE advance in your golf game. How huge? Paraphrasing the immortal words of Neil Armstrong, it's one small step, one giant leap. Here's why:

You now know how far you can hit the ball with each iron in your bag, which is critically important to know when you are playing a round of golf. You'll read more about this in Chapter 20, *Understanding Scorecards And Course Guides.*

If your 100-yard club is the 7-iron, add 10 yards for each club lower than the 7-iron, and subtract 10 yards for each club higher than the 7-iron. Using that formula, estimate that your 6-iron will send the ball about 110 yards; your 5-iron, 120 yards. Going the other way, your 8-iron will send your ball about 90 yards; your 9-iron, about 80 yards.

For women, the difference in distance between each club is typically 10 yards. For men, it's 15 yards.

Woods are used to hit a golf ball farther than irons. Although now made of metal, the club heads were once made out of wood, and the name has stuck even after the technological advancements. Occasionally, you might hear someone call them "metal woods" or "fairway metals."

There are generally three kinds of woods: **drivers, fairway woods**, and **hybrids**. The Driver is considered the 1-wood. It's the longest club in your bag and, for most golfers, the hardest club to control. The most common fairway woods are the 3-wood, 5-wood and 7-wood. And, yes, you use them on the fairway as well as on the teeing ground. In fact, most new golfers hit with a 3-wood off the tee because it's easier to control than the Driver.

Hybrid clubs combine the characteristics of woods and irons. They can be used off the tee and in the fairway. And, should you find yourself in the **rough** (the grass not in the fairway), you'll often find it easier to hit with your hybrid club than with

a wood or an iron. If your set has a hybrid club or two, then it will probably not have one of the lower lofted irons, such as a 4, 5, or 6-iron.

At the driving range, after hitting balls with your irons, hit a few balls off a tee using your hybrid club(s). Then, hit some with your 3- and 5-woods and perhaps a few more with your Driver.

When you feel that you've hit enough balls for one day, but still have some remaining, just leave them for the next golfer. It's an act of kindness that's always appreciated (although golf courses see it as a revenue loss).

*P*ractice (Range) Balls — Practice balls are either "seconds" that the manufacturer's quality control mechanism rejected or they are balls made specifically for driving range use. Some are even distance controlled. They are suitable for practice, but never play with them on the golf course — they will make you look bad in every imaginable way.

"Drive For Show, Putt For Dough."

You'll hear this expression a million times, and that's fine. It underscores one of the great truths about golf: approximately half of your shots in a round of golf will be putts and short shots made from close to the green. It's true even for the pros. If you can improve your putting (and it's the easiest thing to improve!), it will help build your confidence. (And you thought miniature golf was just for goofing around!)

Be sure to allow time for working on your short game — **chipping**, **pitching** and putting. This is where you can make the biggest difference in your game.

*P*ractice facilities vary greatly. Some have only a driving range, while others have a range and a putting green. Still others have both and also a green for chipping and **bunker** practice. Before you start putting, be sure you aren't on the chipping green — you'll be bombarded!

Gail Grace
President
Sunrise Bank

"I started playing in the mid-1980s when I saw the strong connection between business and golf and realized I needed to get in the game, so to speak. To me it seemed a matter of professional survival. My first experience was playing in a scramble with borrowed clubs, and we got a trophy!"

(And she's won a lot of trophies since then — Gail's office is filled with trophies and framed photos of her tournament foursomes. A special treasure is a framed Moon Valley Country Club flag signed by Annika Sorenstam the day she carded a tournament-record 59 there.)

Chapter 6

Scheduling (Reserving) A Tee Time

"A ship in a harbor is safe,
but that is not what ships are built for."

~ William Shedd

New golfers often say that once they get on the golf course and actually play, that's when they realize they love the game. You're ready to find out if that's true for you. You've been practicing. You're comfortable with your clubs and relatively comfortable with your swing. You feel ready to have a go at playing a round of golf with two or three friends. All you need now is a tee time.

Reserving tee times is *reeeeeeeeally* easy. You can do it in person, by phone or online. Online options include your local golf course's website and online golf services such as *golfnow.com* and *golfhub.com*.

Before you attempt to reserve your tee time, determine how many golfers will be in your group. The maximum number allowed is usually four, or a foursome. (My first outing, as part of a fivesome, is quite rare.) Often you will find that courses don't want to reserve a tee time for a party of one. Also note that if you book a tee time for a twosome, the course will very likely put one or two other golfers with you when you arrive. Ideally, a group of four friends is the way to go — especially when you are just learning to play.

Tee times are typically spaced 8 -10 minutes apart, so if you want to play at, say, noon, you may get an 11:52 a.m. time or a 12:08 p.m. time if noon is unavailable. During the busy season, the course may be booked completely, in which case you will have to try a different course or a different day. Fridays, Saturdays and Sundays are the busiest days.

Pay close attention to the EXACT time that is reserved for you, and be sure to tell your playing partners the EXACT tee time. You'll see why this is so important when you get to the next chapter.

When you book your tee time online, be sure to check the course's website for special offers. Many courses offer discounted green fees to customers who book online and occasionally offer breakfast/golf or golf/lunch promotions. One disadvantage of booking online, however, is that you don't have an opportunity to ask what condition the course is in. Necessary seasonal maintenance such as **punching** won't close the course, but it can certainly detract from your playing enjoyment.

Cancelling Your Tee Time – Most courses allow you to cancel your tee time without penalty if you give 24 hours' notice. Always check the course's cancellation policy, particularly with regard to RAIN. If it rains and you don't show up for your tee time, you MAY get charged the full amount.

It will take you approximately 4.5 hours to play 18 holes of golf.

Helen Burland
Owner
Burland Jewelers

"I used to be just a vacation player. I would ride in the cart with my husband and, if we came to a hole I could hit on, I'd get out and hit or putt.

"My husband has been playing since he was young. One day he said that if I'd take up golf, we could join a club — it didn't make sense to join a club for just one person. So I started playing.

"I love the game and love the people I play with. The camaraderie is wonderful. On the golf course, I don't think about anything other than hitting the $%#&! ball — not my house, not my business, not the kids. Golf takes me away from everything."

Chapter

I'm On
A Golf Course!

"Life is no brief candle to me. It is a sort of splendid
torch which I have got a hold of for the moment,
and I want to make it burn as brightly as possible before
handing it on to future generations."

~ George Bernard Shaw

This is the day! For the first time, you are going to play 9 or 18 holes.
Excited?

Your tee time is 12:08 p.m. The **starter** will give you about 5
minutes notice. 12:08 p.m. is the exact time you are expected to hit
your first ball. (If there is no starter, you are expected to be on the
tee at your designated time.) You'll want to warm up before you
play, and you'll need a little time to pay your green fee, shop in the
pro shop, grab something from the snack bar and get your group
together, so ARRIVE AT THE COURSE ABOUT 45 MINUTES
BEFORE YOUR TEE TIME.

The Bag Drop

When you arrive at the golf course, look for a **Bag Drop** sign near
the entrance to the clubhouse. This is where you stop long enough

to give your clubs to one of the attendants before parking your car. The attendant will welcome you, ask for your name and tee time, then put your clubs on a cart . Be sure to ask the attendant where your clubs will be when you exit the pro shop. At the end of your round it is appropriate to tip the attendant a few dollars for this service, but it isn't required. Note that private courses might not allow any tipping.

Some golf courses have locker rooms where you can change into your golf shoes, put on sunscreen, etc. Many do not have locker rooms, however, so you may change into your golf shoes at your car.

The Pro Shop

The friendliest people on earth work in golf course pro shops. They are absolutely committed to helping YOU have a great time at their facility because they want you to come back, and they hope you'll tell others about it. Enjoy the attention!

Someone behind the counter will check you in. Be sure to save your receipt and put it where you can find it — the starter may ask to see it when you are called to the first tee.

If you are riding, the green fee covers the cost of the cart. If you are walking, the green fee will be less. Some courses discourage walking because the distance between holes can be quite long. Some courses may have pull carts that walking golfers can rent for a nominal fee as an alternative to carrying their bags. If you want to hit some practice balls before you play, there may be a small cost for a basket or bag of warm-up balls.

Do you have plenty of golf balls in your bag? A towel? Sunscreen? A glove? A divot repair tool? A ball marker? Now's the time to get anything you need.

Waiting To Tee Off

You'll probably want to hit a few balls to warm up, and you should practice putting, too, to get a feel for how your ball will roll on the short, putting green grass. This is an ideal time for you to count your golf clubs. Be sure that you have all of them and that you do not have more than 14.

About 5 minutes before your tee time, you should be in your cart and ready to go. If you are driving the cart, you will keep score, because the scorecard is on the steering wheel. As a new golfer, however, you have enough going on as it is, so try to let someone else drive the cart and keep score. You'll read about keeping score in Chapter 8, *Understanding Scorecards And Course Guides*. (Relax — keeping score is easy!)

A Few Words About Golf Course Etiquette

This is the topic many beginning golfers are most concerned about, but let me put you at ease. Golf etiquette can be summed up in two words: be courteous. As a new golfer, the most courteous thing you can do is maintain a good pace of play and not hold anyone else back from having a great day on the course. Keeping up a fast or reasonable pace of play is the one thing on the golf course that is totally within your control. This will also be the biggest factor in your popularity with your playing partners.

When a player in your group is preparing to hit her ball, position yourself behind her and to the side, outside her peripheral vision. (Think "bellies to backsides.") Remain still and quiet — you don't want to distract her or be the scapegoat should she make a "special" shot. When she hits her ball, watch where it goes so you can help locate it.

Most private golf clubs forbid the use of cell phones on the course, and most golfers, whether playing a private course or a public one, turn their phones OFF. In other words, be in the moment and be with your group. If you absolutely must check your messages, do it at **the turn**.

The key ring on the cart may have two keys. The bigger key is for the rest rooms (comfort stations! Yeah!) on the course.

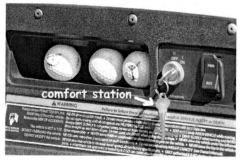

The golf cart has an ON/ OFF key and a forward-reverse control. This control may be a switch on the cart's dashboard or a lever on the seat bench between you and your playing partner.

To make the cart go, step on the accelerator. There is no need to turn the key on and off. When you stop the cart, be sure to lock the brake by depressing the top portion of the brake pedal until it clicks.

When you stop your cart behind another cart, as you will do each time you reach the teeing ground for the next hole, always leave enough room between the carts to allow the front cart's golfers easy access to their clubs.

The starter at the golf course or the staff in the staging area will usually tell you where you may and may not drive the cart. Sometimes you'll see a notice on the golf cart itself. Here are some common guidelines you may see:

- Cart path only (typical when the course conditions are very wet or shortly after **overseeding**).
- 90-degree rule — drive on the cart path, and when you near your ball, turn 90 degrees to approach it. After hitting, drive back to the cart path the way you came.
- Scatter rule — you may drive anywhere in any direction.

Ann Lieff
Account Manager, People Solutions,
HKMB HUB International

"I never thought I would say these words: I love golf! Today I confess I love everything about it. The fresh air, the varying topography, the walking, the Saturday morning camaraderie with my girlfriends, the rounds played with colleagues, clients or my husband, the fashion and outfits--and most of all, the challenge of the game. A game you can play practically anywhere in the world! Looking back a few years, I know one of the main reasons I decided to take up golf was because I thought I would like to see my husband in retirement. Another confession: At the end of the day, I have to say, I love the game for ME!"

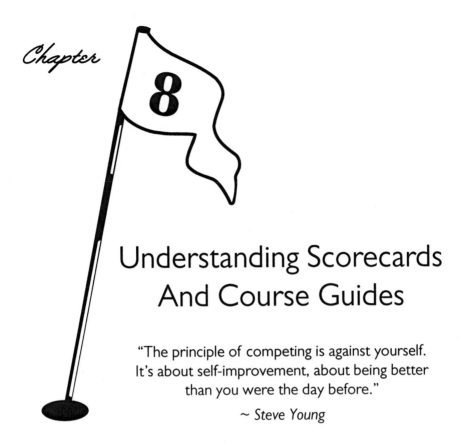

Understanding Scorecards
And Course Guides

"The principle of competing is against yourself.
It's about self-improvement, about being better
than you were the day before."

~ Steve Young

The key to your golf game is your 100-yard club, and the key to the golf course is the scorecard. Here's why:

> The scorecard tells you everything you need to know about the course — how long each hole is, how difficult each hole is compared to all the other holes, how difficult the course is compared to all other courses, and how to make the scoring fair for each player in your group. The scorecard also informs you of any "Local Rules," such as what is considered out of bounds. It even gives the golf course's phone number, should you need it.

Take a look at the Scottsdale Silverado Golf Club scorecard. Reading from top to bottom, this is what it tells us:

> The course has 3 sets of tees for each hole — gold, white and red. Rating/Slope, given for each Tee, is an overall measure of the difficulty of the course, played from each respective tee.

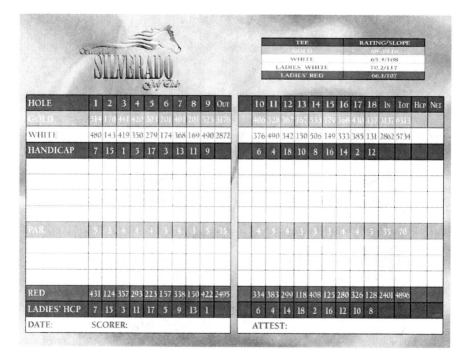

TEE	RATING/SLOPE
GOLD	68.0/116
WHITE	65.4/108
LADIES' WHITE	70.2/117
LADIES' RED	66.3/107

HOLE	1	2	3	4	5	6	7	8	9	Out	10	11	12	13	14	15	16	17	18	In	Tot	Hcp	Net
GOLD	514	170	441	420	303	201	401	201	523	3176	400	328	367	167	533	179	368	430	137	3137	6313		
WHITE	480	143	419	350	279	174	368	169	490	2872	376	490	342	150	506	149	333	385	131	2862	5734		
HANDICAP	7	15	1	5	17	3	13	11	9		6	4	18	10	8	16	14	2	12				
PAR	5	3	4	4	4	3	4	3	5	35	4	5	4	3	5	3	4	4	5	35	70		
RED	431	124	357	293	223	157	338	150	422	2495	334	383	299	118	408	125	280	326	128	2401	4896		
LADIES' HCP	7	15	3	11	17	5	9	13	1		6	4	14	18	2	16	12	10	8				

DATE: SCORER: ATTEST:

The next line down is "Hole." Note that after 9 is the word "Out," and after 18 is the word "In," followed by "Tot(al)," "Hcp," and "Net."

- "Out" is your score for the first 9 holes.

- "In" is your score for holes 10 through 18.

- "Tot" is the sum of "Out" and "In" (your **gross score**).

- "Hcp" is your **handicap**.

- "Net" is your score after your handicap is subtracted from your gross score.

The next line down, "Gold," tells golfers playing from the gold tee how long each hole is. The first hole, No. 1, is 514 yards.

The "White" line and the "Red" line show the length of each hole for golfers playing from the white and red tees.

Below the "White" line is the "Handicap" line (for the gold and white tees), and below the "Red" line is the "Ladies Handicap" information. Look at the numbers in each of these lines. Hole handicaps rank each hole from most to least difficult.

The most difficult hole on the course for players playing from the gold or white tee is Hole No. 3. It is the "1" handicap hole.

The most difficult hole on the course for players playing from the red tee is No. 9. See the "1?"

The **par** line tells you what the expected score for a skilled player is on each hole. Hole No. 1 is a par 5, for example. No. 2 is a par-3. Hole No. 3 is a par 4. To avoid putting pressure on yourself when you are first learning to play, don't be all that concerned with your score. Keeping score is fun as your skills improve and you begin challenging yourself to get around the course with the fewest shots possible.

*B*enchmarks – As a new golfer, sometimes it's tough to keep an accurate score. This is especially true if you're picking up your ball and dropping it near/on the green in order to finish the hole with the rest of your group.

Even if this is the case, you can still keep score and can also set some goals for yourself by counting your putts. For example, you can note on the scorecard the number of putts you take on each hole. Another thing to count might be the number of "feel good" shots — shots that go where you intended. These can give you benchmarks on important elements of your golf game.

The blank lines are for recording scores. Write each player's name in the boxes on the left, and enter each player's score after every hole. (Record the scores when you reach the teeing area for the next hole. This helps keep things moving for everyone on the course, and it will minimize your chances of being hit by a ball played from the group behind you.)

At the bottom of the scorecard is a place to write the date, the name of the player who kept score, and the name of the player who checked all the addition and attests that the scores are accurate. This is important mainly when you are playing in an event that requires you to turn in your scorecard.

On the reverse side of the scorecard are the Local Rules you need to know and some other information that may be helpful — the phone number for the Pro Shop, etc.

Handicaps

The purpose of the Golf Canada Handicap and the USGA Handicap systems is to make the game of golf enjoyable by enabling golfers of differing abilities to compete on an equitable basis. The handicap reflects your "potential" and not your actual average score. In Canada, to establish a Handicap Factor®, you may either belong to a golf club OR you may join your provincial golf association as a Public Players Club member. Find out more by visiting www.golfcanada.ca. In the United States, according to USGA rules, you must belong to a golf club in order to maintain a USGA Handicap Index. Most tournaments in the United States that use handicaps require that you have a USGA Handicap Index. If you want to play in one of these tournaments or if you're interested in getting a handicap index, ask someone in your local pro shop if the Club offers handicap services.

Your golf handicap index is generated by a formula based on your last 20 rounds and your 10 best scores in those rounds. You can establish a handicap with as few as 5 18-hole rounds, 10 9-hole rounds, or a combination of the two — so long as you play these rounds under the Rules of Golf.

Course Guides Or Yardage Books

Course guides are booklets or two-sided cards that provide pictures and details for each hole. They vary in quality and level of detail from one course to another, and some courses don't offer them at all. Many courses include a diagram of each hole on the scorecard.

Upscale courses give each player a booklet with either a photograph or an illustration of each hole. Distances to sand bunkers and water hazards are shown, as are distances from various spots on the fairway to the green. Some guides even offer tips on how to play each hole.

Global Positioning System (GPS) technology has a very large presence in the world of golf. More and more courses have golf carts with GPS monitors that provide you with detailed information on the placement of and distance to various features on the course. GPS monitors definitely speed up the pace of play because they provide the information you need to quickly determine which club to hit and which direction to go. Personal GPS devices are also becoming commonplace.

Kate Rakoci
CEO and Founder
Jack Of All Trades

"Do I wish I could play better? Of course. When people ask how my golf game is I say, 'Well, it's mine.' Having a golf game is what is important. Not how you play, nor how often, nor with whom. Just have a golf game. It does wonders for your social life and business life alike. Or at least it can, if you let it. Have I made mistakes in business? None that a mulligan wouldn't have fixed."

Chapter 9

We're Up — Let's Play Some Golf!

"Treat everyone you meet as though they're the most important person you'll meet that day."

~ Roger Dawson

On a warm and sunny day, when cotton-ball clouds float lazily on the sky, and the grass has been cut, and every fragrant flower in the world is blooming nearby, and you're hanging with three friends… and it's a weekday…you wonder why you didn't take up golf much sooner in life.

The great thing is, you DID take it up, and now you're about to play your first round. You hear something like this:

"Now on the number one tee, Scottsdale Silverado Golf Club welcomes the (Your name) foursome. Ladies, whenever you're ready."

You and your foursome (let's name your three friends Barbara, Connie and Diane) decide to play from the Forward (Red) tees. Each of you has marked your ball with a permanent marker — a dot or

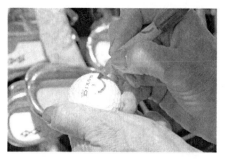

a line or your initial, something that identifies it as your ball. You have decided who will hit first, second, third and last. A common way to determine your hitting order is to flip a tee into the air: whoever it points to when it lands plays first, and so on. (On all holes after the first one, the player with the lowest score on the previous hole has the **honors** and hits first.)

NOTE: *When players in the same group are playing from different tee markers (two players playing Red and two players playing from the White Tees, for example) the "Back" (White) Tee plays first. Think safety!*

Wouldn't you know it? The tee landed pointing at you, so you're up!

You know from looking at the Silverado scorecard that this first hole is a par 5 and 431 yards long, Red Tee to the center of the green. You want your ball to go as far as possible on your tee shot, so you choose to hit your Driver or, if you feel more confident with it, your 3-wood. So far, so good.

You are allowed to tee up your ball using a wooden or plastic tee ONLY ON YOUR TEE SHOTS — in other words, only on the first shot for each hole that you hit from the teeing ground.

two club lengths

Where To Tee Up Your Ball

Look at the teeing ground. At the front of it are two red markers. You may tee up your ball anywhere behind and between those markers. You may go behind them as much as two club lengths and within two club lengths of an imaginary line connecting them.

There's no need to be nervous about being first to hit — but many, many golfers confess they ARE nervous about it, so welcome to the club! Just take a deep breath, envision a beautiful shot and swing away! Watch your ball so you know where to find it.

Placing the Tee in the Ground and the Ball on the Tee

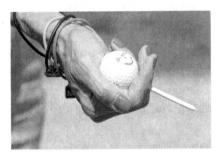

One of the easiest ways to place the tee into the ground (and look like you know what you're doing) is to start by holding the ball in the palm of your hand. At the same time, place a tee in your hand with the large round top of the tee between your index and middle fingers, and hold it so that the ball is touching the top part of the tee. Holding the ball and tee together, place the tip of the tee in the ground. Press down on the ball (and, therefore, on the tee at the same time) with your palm to get the tee into the ground at the height you want. And there you are — the ball will already be on the tee! According to Arizona State University's women's golf coach, Melissa Luellen, using the pressure from your palm rather than your fingers to sink the tee into the ground will also save many a broken fingernail!

As each player tees off, the other three players remain quiet and still, out of peripheral view, and watch the flight of the ball. It is quite acceptable to compliment a player who hits a good shot.

How High To Tee Your Ball

When hitting the ball off the tee with a wood, set your club head on the ground behind the ball. The general rule of thumb is that at least half of the ball should appear above the crown of your club head. The goal is to position the ball in line with the "sweet

spot" on the club. If you tee the ball too high, then when you swing, the club might go underneath the ball, popping it high into the air and advancing it far less than you anticipated. When hitting the ball with an iron, tee the ball up only slightly so that it looks inviting to hit.

Hitting A Provisional Ball

"Special" shots happen!

When a player hits a shot that appears to go out of bounds or may not be findable, she should hit a provisional ball from the same spot. Let's imagine that Barbara hooks her tee shot into the desert area along the left side of the fairway. White stakes mark the out-of-bounds line.

It appears that her ball might be **OB**, but Barbara is not sure. There is always the chance that the ball hit a rock or something and bounced back into the fairway. It would be safely in play in this case. But since Barbara is unsure whether the ball is in or out of bounds, she must declare (say aloud) that she is hitting a provisional ball. If her first ball is OB, she will play her provisional ball (assuming that the provisional ball is in bounds). Your foursome can now proceed to your next shots.

NOTE: Hitting the provisional ball when in doubt helps maintain your pace of play. There is nothing that hurts pace of play (and your pride!) more than having to go all the way back to the tee (where another group may be waiting!) to hit another ball after you discover that your first ball is lost or OB.

High fives all around, ladies! You're off!

After hitting your tee shot, be sure to pick up your wooden or plastic tee for reuse. If it is broken, pick up the pieces and discard them in the designated container or, if one is not present, leave them next to the tee marker.

Some golf courses provide a bucket of divot repair mixture on the tee so players can fill in their divots. There is usually a container of this material with each golf cart, too, so you can fill in fairway divots. And no, these containers are not for cigarette butts.

Robyn Nordin Stowell
Golf and Private Club Attorney with National Practice

"I started playing golf with my husband for fun. We would play late in the summer day — a few bucks for as many holes as you could finish before sundown (that was about the right price for how I played then).

"Years later, I started playing regularly with women and learned that the fun, good company, scenery, and fresh air were more important than the score. I enjoyed tournament play where I felt pressure to play well, and was also happy to play for fun with a group that just picked up their bad shots. I realize the latter is not really playing golf, but it is enjoying friends and colleagues on the golf course, which in some cases is just perfect. It is crucial, however, to know the difference and to follow the customs and etiquette of golf when appropriate.

"I learned a lesson in graciousness from a scratch golfer in my business foursome when he announced on the first tee that, because this was not the US Open, he hoped no one would mind if he had a horrible shot, he picked up his ball or tossed it into the fairway. Of course, he was not going to have ANY bad shots, but we all were relaxed and had more fun because he (the best golfer of us) set the tone that this was for fun. We ended up sticking pretty close to the rules anyway, but it was very gracious on his part. When the day comes that I am by far the best golfer in my foursome, I hope I will be that gracious myself (and even before then, in smaller ways).

"Currently, I love to head out for a game of 9 or 18 holes with my clients, colleagues, friends and even my daughters! I have deepened relationships and friendships in a relaxed environment. And it's true: you really do learn a lot about a person by playing golf with them."

Chapter

10

Welcome To
Your First Fairway!

"The potential of the average person is like a huge
ocean unsailed, a new continent unexplored,
a world of possibilities waiting to be released and
channeled toward some great good."

~ Brian Tracy

For the sake of simplicity, let's assume Barbara is your cart partner.
You drive to the spot where you last saw her ball and stop to look
for the ball in the desert. Always take a golf club with you when you
are looking for a ball, so you can retrieve the ball if it is under a bush
or hard to reach.

After a couple of minutes of looking, you find that Barbara's ball is
indeed out of bounds. You then go either to her provisional ball or
your ball, whichever one is FARTHEST FROM THE GREEN. In golf,
the player who is farthest from the target (the hole marked with the
flag on the green) hits first.

Your tee shot went farther than Barbara's provisional ball, so she will
hit before you play your second shot.

Because her first ball could not be found, Barbara is playing her
provisional ball, and she now "lies 3." Here's why: her first stroke

was the shot off the tee, her second stroke was actually a penalty stroke, and when she hit the provisional ball it was her third stroke. The next ball she hits will be her fourth stroke. After Barbara hits, you proceed to your ball and assess your situation. Well done — your ball is in the middle of the fairway!

First, look at the ball without touching it to confirm it is your ball. You "lie 1." The next ball you hit

*R**eady golf** helps maintain a proper pace of play. Normally the player farthest from the hole hits first, but in ready golf, it's whoever is ready to hit. You can play ready golf off the tee, in the fairway or around the green. Just make sure that your playing partners have agreed to play ready golf and aren't in danger of being hit by your ball.*

will be your second stroke. But how far is it to the green? Which club should you hit? You need to determine where you are, but how?

Every golf course provides key distance markers to help you calculate which club to use for each shot. Most fairways are marked in the middle with indicators at the 100-yard distance, the 150-yard distance, the 200-yard distance and, on longer holes, the 250-yard distance. Also, these same distances may be marked on the cart paths. To determine your distance from one of these markers, pace it off. For a person of average height, a slightly longer than normal step is about one yard.

Sprinkler heads can often help you too. Find a nearby sprinkler head. There is a number on it. Let's say you find one right by your ball and the number on it is "281." Here's what you now know:

You are about 280 yards from the center of the green. (Nice drive — you hit it about 150 yards!)

This is a par 5 hole, so ideally you'd like to be on the green

with your third shot. This would put you on the green **in regulation**, i.e., in position to make a 1-putt **birdie** or a 2-putt par.

About 130 yards ahead, there is a very large fairway bunker on the right side of the fairway. How do you know it is 130 yards to the bunker?

In the middle of the fairway ahead of you is a black and white pole. This pole is 150 yards from the center of the green. The sand bunker is approximately even with the pole. Voila! — 280 minus 150 is 130.

To get safely past the bunker you need to hit your second shot 140 yards, which may be pushing it at this stage of your skill development. You should keep this in mind when making your club selection, and aim to hit your ball to the middle of the fairway (away from the bunker). If you do this, you will "take the bunker out of play." Then you will be ready for your third shot, with the goal being to hit your ball onto the green in regulation.

What color is the flag on the green? Most golf courses use the American Golf red/white/blue system. A red flag means the hole is in the front third of the green; a white flag indicates the hole is in the middle of the green; and a blue flag indicates the hole is in the back third of the green. Depending on flag color, you might need to add or subtract 5 - 10 yards when calculating how far you want to hit your approach shot. Similarly, in the fairway, you might see a red indicator for the 100-yard distance, a white indicator for the 150-yard distance, and a blue indicator for the 200-yard distance.

Envision your shot each time, take a practice swing and then swing away!

The four of you continue to advance to the green, taking turns according to whose ball is farthest from the target, which today is marked with a red flag.

As you get closer, notice the "Carts" signs in the fairway. The arrows on these signs direct you to the cart path, as you are not allowed to drive your cart on the fairway as you approach the green. If a player's ball is sitting between these markers and the green, it may make sense for the player to grab her putter and a few clubs and walk the rest of the way to her ball and then to the green. If she does this, make sure the other player takes the cart to the green-side cart path. If, after you putt, you have to run back and retrieve the cart, it will slow the pace of play.

Extra Clubs Help Pace Of Play – On occasion, a golf course will ask you to keep the carts on the cart paths for the entire round. To help maintain a good pace of play when you have to walk to your ball and aren't sure what kind of lie you have or how far you will need to hit, **bracket** your club selection. For example, if you think you will need a 7-iron, take your 8-iron and your 6-iron, too. That way you have it covered. You may also want to take your putter so you can walk straight to the green without having to come back to the cart.

Edythe L. Higgins
Vice President, Business Development Officer
Wells Fargo

"My boss said I had to play in the 'Fresh Start' golf tournament because our company was an Elite level sponsor. I quickly took a lesson at Phoenix Country Club beforehand so that I'd know how to hold the handle. But the reason we Wells Fargo women started playing regularly is because we saw all the guys leaving during the day to play golf — and the bank was sponsoring their participation. Duh!

"Aside from simply doing something that is fun, I've found that golf is good for my business relationships — either to thank customers or to obtain new ones."

The Green And Your Short Game

"Never let the fear of striking out get in your way."

~ *George Herman "Babe" Ruth*

The green is truly happy land, the place every player is trying to get to. It's the big target that surrounds the bulls-eye — the hole marked by a red, white or blue flag. If you reach the green in regulation, you've hit some great shots to get there—and on occasion, lucky shots, too! When you aren't quite on the green in regulation, the most important part of your golf game comes into play: your short game.

The short game is a term golfers use when they are referring to **chipping**, **pitching** and **putting**. These are the kinds of shots you'll be using around and on the green. To help explain this part of the game, imagine that this is the situation when your foursome reaches the green:

> You have hit three tremendous shots and find your ball sitting on the green approximately 20' past the hole. (Way to go!)

***M**ark Your Ball On The Green so your playing partners have a clear view of their putts. You may use anything for a marker — a lucky coin, the removable marker that comes on some golf gloves, or a plastic disk. The overwhelming majority of players put the*

marker behind the ball, and you should, too, but you can put it on either side or in front of the ball. Just be consistent about it because you'll incur a penalty if you fail to put your ball back EXACTLY WHERE IT WAS. Also, if your marker is in another player's putting line and she asks you to move it left or right, move your marker the length of one putter head in this way:

- Set the heel of your putter on the green, right next to your marker; then

- Position your putter head so that it points to a stationary object, such as a tree; then

- Move your marker the length of one putter head — NOT the length of your putter. If you place your marker upside down at the end of the putter head, it will remind you that you will need to move it back before you can putt.

Be sure to reverse this procedure exactly to re-position your marker when it is your turn to putt.

Barbara's ball is in the greenside bunker on the left side of the green.

Connie finds her ball on fluffy grass, to the right of the green, but there is a greenside bunker between her ball and the green.

Diane's ball is nestled on a grassy mound just beyond the back of the green.

Who plays first? Diane is farthest from the hole, so she plays first. Before she plays, however, you should mark your ball's location with a coin or marker. After you mark your ball, move to the side of the green, out of her path and line of vision.

Diane uses a wedge to execute a little chip shot. A chip is like a putt but with a low-flying start. Her goal is to get the ball out of the grass and rolling on the green toward the hole. Diane's ball stops just short of your ball marker. She marks her ball with a ball marker before the next player plays.

Connie is farther from the hole than Barbara, so she hits next. She will have to execute a pitch shot up and over the bunker using a higher-lofted club such as her pitching wedge, sand wedge or lob wedge. If she does this properly, her ball will land softly and safely on the green. She succeeds and her ball stops within a few feet of the flagstick in the hole, also called the "flag" or "pin." (Great shot, Connie!)

Barbara is the only player not yet on the green. She enters the bunker, taking a rake with her (to help keep the pace of play moving). She manages to get her ball out of the sand and onto the green using a sand wedge, but the ball rolls across the green and into the grass on the other side.

NOTE: **Grounding** your club in a bunker results in a two-stroke penalty. Your club cannot touch the sand for any reason before you take your shot. Nor can you move any natural objects in the bunker — a twig, a pinecone or a leaf, for example. However, if your ball is sitting next to, say, a paper cup that has blown into the bunker, you may remove the cup because it is artificial. The same goes for the rake, but be careful to lift the rake from the sand without dragging it — dragging it would suggest that you are testing the sand in some way, and you'll incur a penalty. After hitting your ball out of the bunker, rake the sand so that there is no evidence you were there, i.e., leave it smooth.

After Barbara rakes the bunker to erase her tracks, she can play her next shot. While you are waiting for her to get to her ball, repair any ball marks you see, especially any that your ball might have made when it landed on the green.

When Barbara is ready to play, she elects to use her putter even though her ball is not on the green. And, because it isn't on the green, she has the choice of keeping the flagstick in the hole or having it pulled out. Many players in this situation prefer to keep the flagstick in, because if they hit the ball too firmly but on the right line, the flagstick will stop the ball from rolling too far past the hole.

Barbara's ball stops about six feet from the hole.

Connie is closest to the hole so she **tends the flag.** (Before pulling out the flagstick, she asks whether everyone can see the hole.) Diane putts first because she is farthest away.

How to Tend and Remove the Flag

- Give it a little twist as you're pulling it out, which makes it easier. Be careful to avoid hitting the edge of the cup when you remove the flagstick and when you put it back in.

- Place the flagstick on the ground away from where any

player will be putting so that it isn't a distraction and can't be hit by an errant putt (incurring a two-stroke penalty).

- Always lay the flagstick on the green gently — tossing it or dropping it could dent the putting surface or damage the grass.

- Generally, the player who holes out first (i.e., gets her ball in the hole) takes responsibility for replacing the flagstick in the hole once all of the players in the group have finished. If it's easier for someone else to do it, no problem, especially if it helps the pace of play.

3 Steps To Reading The Green

Greens typically have some slope or undulation, which allows the water to drain properly and helps the golf course architect give golfers a little extra challenge. Being a good putter requires understanding how the ball will curve, slow down, or speed up as it heads to the hole. Sometimes it might curve in both directions, or go up and down more than once.

1. As you approach the green from the fairway or cart path, take advantage of the opportunity to view the topography of the green and how it might affect the path of your ball once you hit it toward the hole. How is the green sloped?

2. When you're standing behind your ball, ask yourself, "If I poured a glass of water onto the green, which way would the water run?" If you're putting uphill, the ball will travel more slowly and have less break than if you are putting downhill. Remember, the law of gravity prevails!

3. It's helpful to pay attention when your playing partners attempt their putts. Notice the direction and speed the balls travel, especially when they are close to the hole.

Courtesy Around The Green

Even for skilled players, putting can be intense — after all, a 2-foot putt counts the same as a 250-yard drive! Because of this, play around the green requires specific etiquette. Some of the key aspects are:

Heed The "Sacred Ground:" There's an imaginary line between another player's ball and the hole. NEVER STEP ON THIS LINE! It's best to walk around the outside of your playing partner's ball or ball marker so you don't step on the imaginary line. If you're sure you're not going to violate the space, you may step gingerly over it. There's no penalty for stepping on someone's line, but it makes you look inconsiderate and ignorant, and it certainly doesn't endear you to your playing partners.

Where To Stand: The imaginary line also has implications for where you should stand while waiting your turn. You shouldn't stand in any other player's line. This includes the line that extends behind her and directly across from her on the other side of the hole.

Know Your Shadow: You don't want your shadow to cross anyone's line, so be sure to keep yourself positioned appropriately. This is especially noteworthy early and late in the day when shadows can be quite long.

Putting Order Options: If your ball is farthest from the hole, you are considered to be **away** or **out**. You would putt first. If you don't make your putt, you may ask your playing partners if they'd mind if you finish. This is one way of maintaining your group's pace of play. There are a few reasons you may choose NOT to continue:

- You'd be standing in another player's line.
- You want time to line up your next putt.

- You want to "regroup" from a "special" putt and need time to refocus.

If this is the case, mark your ball and be ready to play your shot promptly when it's time.

How To Repair A Ball Mark

*Ball marks (you might also hear them referred to as **pitch marks**) are indentations caused when a ball lands on the green. Unrepaired ball marks can take two to three weeks to properly heal, leaving behind an unsightly and uneven putting surface. A repaired ball mark takes less than half that time to heal.*

As a steward of the game, fix your ball mark and any others you see while your partners are putting. The rule of thumb is to fix your mark and one other.

There's really not much to it:

- *Use a divot repair tool or a tee;*
- *Insert it at the edges of the ball mark - not the middle of the depression;*
- *Bring the edges together with a gentle twisting motion, but don't lift the center – you don't want to tear the roots;*
- *Gently tap the surface with the bottom of your putter or your foot;*

You're done when it's a surface you would want to putt over.

tap it down

Before You Leave The Green

Check to make sure your foursome has picked up all the clubs that were brought to the green. One good way to avoid leaving clubs behind is to place any extra clubs next to the flagstick after it is pulled. Or, leave them at the edge of the green where you will see them easily on your way back to the golf carts.

Lana Hock
First Vice President
The Hoffman and Hock Group
Robert W. Baird & Co.

"I hired a life coach whose background was in sports psychology. During one of our sessions he asked whether I played golf. I'd hit a few balls before, but that's about it. So he said we should have a session at a golf course, because it would be fun and it's a great place to get to know someone. He said, in a round of golf, everyone becomes who they are, that it all comes out. We went and I hit a few good shots along with the bad shots. He helped me believe I could do it, and I stuck with it.

"A major source of business for me is referrals, so I tend to golf a lot with business colleagues, more so than with clients. I don't like to talk business when I am golfing with a client, but I DO talk business when golfing with colleagues. We have some common ground. Sometimes I can help them with a client need, and sometimes they can help me. There's a lot of cross-promotion.

"I try to play in at least one charity golf event per month. It's fun, and it's an opportunity to give something back to the community."

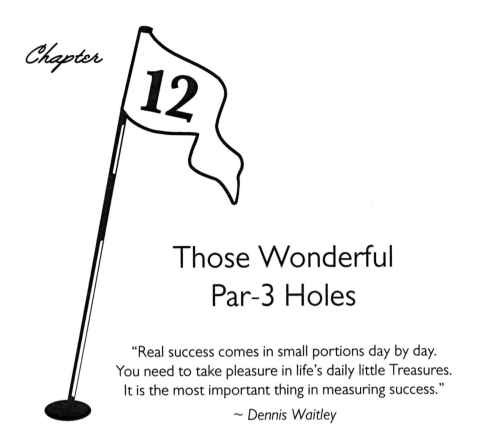

12

Those Wonderful
Par-3 Holes

"Real success comes in small portions day by day.
You need to take pleasure in life's daily little Treasures.
It is the most important thing in measuring success."

~ *Dennis Waitley*

Most golfers welcome the opportunity to play a par-3 hole during their rounds because par-3s are shorter holes and are reachable in one shot. Most championship-length par 72 courses have four par-3s. But what par-3s lack in distance they make up for in difficulty.

At Scottsdale Silverado Golf Course, the second hole is a 124-yard par-3 from the Forward Tee. As you stand on the tee contemplating which club to use, note the color and location of the flag. Also observe that the green is slightly higher in elevation than the teeing ground that you're standing on, there is a greenside bunker located at the left front of the green, and there is a backstop mound at the back of the green.

The flag is red, and you know that means the hole is located in the front third of the green. The flag is also on the left side of the green, which brings the greenside bunker into play. If your shot is short, there is a very good chance you'll end up in the bunker. This hole location is often called a "sucker pin" because, even though the shorter distance initially makes the hole seem easy, a bunker lies in waiting.

Because the green is elevated slightly, add 5-10 yards to the distance. However, because the flag is red, you'll want to subtract about 10 yards from the distance shown on the scorecard. After you do the math in your head, you determine that you need to choose a club that will send your ball about 120 yards.

Which club do you hit? First, think of which club you use for a shot of 100 yards: your 7-iron. This means your 6-iron should give you a shot of 110 yards or so, and your 5-iron — Voila! — a shot of 120 yards. There is no need to worry about hitting it too long, because there is the mound in the back. The safe play is to aim for the center of the green, because you'll be about the right distance AND you will take the greenside bunker out of play.

After each player hits her tee shot you proceed to the green. Connie has unfortunately hit her ball far to the left. This is about when you notice the "Cart Path Only" or "Keep Carts on Path" signs. Connie must walk to her ball. Uncertain what kind of lie she has, she takes two or three clubs with her, including her putter. There are a couple reasons for taking several clubs when you have to walk across the fairway to reach your ball:

- When you reach your ball, you want to be sure you have the right club so that you don't have to return to the cart before hitting.

- You don't know what kind of lie you have. Is it in deep grass or a divot, or is it okay? Also, what if you hit your shot poorly and your ball lands in the greenside bunker? You may need an additional club for that.

Par-3 holes offer the potential for a **hole-in-one**, arguably the biggest thrill a golfer can experience. But keep in mind that making par on a par-3 is a great score (making par on any hole is a great score!), so playing it safe by aiming for the middle of the green is always a good option.

When To Say "Uncle" And Pick Up

When you are on an airplane flying somewhere and you hear the pilot making an announcement, you listen. So listen to this announcement from Delta Airlines Captain Kim Hinshaw, who, when she isn't flying, is playing golf:

"When I am playing a casual round of golf with friends, my personal rule is to pick up my ball as soon as it becomes obvious that the best I can do is make double par or more on the hole. If I muff a couple shots, for example, I might ask the long driver in the group if she would mind me dropping my ball where hers lies, and playing the rest of the hole from there. Or, I might just drop my ball on the green when the other players in my group have reached the green. I'll putt out for the practice.

"Golf is a game meant to be fun and entertaining, particularly when you're starting out, so do whatever it takes to keep your smile intact. Say 'Uncle' and pick up. You're in a beautiful setting with leisure time to be there. Enjoy every minute and start over on the next hole."

Amy Lynne
Entrepreneurial Management Student

"I am pretty new to golf, but already there are some things I can tell you. One, the more I play, the more often I hit good shots, and the more SAWEET shots I hit, the more self-confidence I have on and off the course. Two, relationships I'm developing through golf (player to ball, player to players, player to self) are shedding light on instinctive reactions I have to certain traits of mine — letting go of the negativity I feel when I hit a poor shot allows me to enjoy the entire round, for example. Three, being perceived as *a golfer* gives me a little boost of confidence. Four, when I am with a bunch of people I don't know, I have discovered a great way to say I am fascinating and approachable: I ask, 'Does anyone else here play golf?'"

Chapter

13

Playing Golf
The Shrek Way
(There's a little Shrek in all of us!)

"Life is made up, not of great sacrifices or duties,
but of little things, in which smiles and kindness,
and small obligations win and preserve the heart."

~ Humphrey Davy

An awkward aspect of taking up golf later in life is that you look like an adult, and aren't adults supposed to look like they know what they are doing? But, like Tom Hanks' character in *Big*, the reality is that on the golf course, you're a little kid in a grownup's body —until you *do* know what you are doing.

My son Ben and I discovered our *SHREK* when Ben was taking golf lessons as a youngster. One of the things the instructor wanted his students to learn was golf etiquette. And he told them there would be a test. Seeing that Ben was struggling to remember everything, I sat down with him and together we came up a mnemonic device. (The irony of taking etiquette advice from an ogre! But it sure made it all memorable for a 10-year-old boy.)

Here's what we put together, modified a bit for an adult audience:

S = Watch out for the *Safety* of others

- Before you take a practice swing or a real swing, look around and make sure no one is close to you.
- Don't hit your ball if there's a chance you might hit someone in your group or in the group ahead of you — golf balls don't always go where we want them to, particularly when you're starting out.
- If you think your ball is going to hit someone, yell "Fore!" immediately and loudly.

H = *Help* your partners and other golfers

- If someone forgets a golf club on the ground, pick it up and hand it to her.
- Watch where your partner's ball goes, and help her search for it if it doesn't land in the fairway.
- Repair your divots in the fairway, fix your ball marks on the green and smooth the sand in the bunkers.

R = *Really* forgive others

- If someone makes a noise, talks, or distracts you while you're hitting, don't blame them for your poor shot. Move on to the next one.
- If you're playing a game and a partner lets you down with a bad shot, she's probably already feeling bad. Support her.

E = *Express* gratitude

- Shake hands with your playing partners at the end of your round, thanking them for their company.
- If you're a guest, you can express your gratitude by picking up the first round of beverages on the course, or the first round after golf when you are in the clubhouse — also known as the **19th hole**.

K = *Kindness* is king

- Yes, golf can be frustrating, but watch your language.
- Competition is part of the game, but it takes a back seat to fair play and sportsmanship.

As you can see from the acronym, golf is valuable for building character and teaching life skills to children (and to adults!). Ben did pass his test, by the way.

"Would You Like To Play Through?"

When you are part of a foursome and the group behind you is a twosome, occasionally they have to wait on you. Knowing that someone is waiting on you can feel very uncomfortable. Ask them if they would like to play through or just wave them through. They might even ask you if you'd mind, and that's fine.

If you offer them the opportunity to play through and they accept, move to the side of the fairway or an appropriate location so that you are not in danger of being hit by one of their golf balls.

They will (should!) thank you as they pass by. Wish them a good round and resume playing once they are out of range.

Be mindful that maintaining a good pace of play means that you keep up with the group ahead. So, if you are being pressed by the group behind you, make sure it's because your foursome is waiting on the group ahead of you, not because your foursome is playing slowly. Always focus forward, not back.

Char Carson
LPGA Instructor

"Golf wasn't an instant attraction for me. I had a hard
time understanding why people would pay so much for a
frustrating experience. Besides, I could throw the ball farther
than I could hit it. But, one day, I hit a really good shot and
thought, *Oh! THAT'S why you do it!* I didn't play that often until
I moved from Green Bay to Chicago and didn't know anyone.
Golf became a focal point because it let me meet people. I
could hit it and was comfortable calling up and asking for a
tee time for a single. I'd always get put with three men. Their
shoulders would slump and I knew they were thinking, *Oh,
no. A woman!* And then I'd outdrive them. By the second hole
we'd be exchanging business cards."

Chapter

These Things Happen

"Small improvements in the way you use your time can translate into major differences in your life."

~ Brian Tracy

Golf is a fun game governed by rules of play every player is expected to know. There really aren't that many rules, despite the common perception to the contrary. But golf is renowned for the honesty and sportsmanship that players embrace and expect of one another. Golf is a game of integrity, and golfers are obligated to call penalties on themselves.

If you find yourself wondering whether you can legally do something on the golf course and suspect there is a rule about it, check the Golf Canada and/or USGA (United States Golf Association) Rules of Golf book that you carry in your golf bag. (Yes! Buy one and keep it in your bag. You don't need to read it cover to cover, but keep it handy as a reference tool.) If you are playing in a tournament, ask a tournament official. When playing a casual round of golf with friends, consult your fellow players.

In addition to normal, everyday situations, the Rules of Golf cover all sorts of oddball circumstances, from what happens if an animal steals your ball off the fairway (you replace a ball where it was, no penalty) to what you do if you hit the ball twice in one swing (you count two strokes, one for the shot and one penalty).

When you are learning to play golf, the rules can seem so intimidating they become distracting. While it is true that knowledge is power (and ignorance is bliss!), knowing every rule is not critically important when you are enjoying a round of casual, less structured golf. Recall that my first experience on a golf course included learning how to play a foot wedge!

Once you gain more experience, the rules make more and more sense. Here are some of the most common things beginning golfers ask about and the rules that apply to them. Oh, and to make things easier to understand — because the official rules of golf are technical and dry — they are demystified with simpler language here:

What Happens If My Ball Falls Off The Tee?

- **Rule 11-3 Ball Falling Off Tee**

   If you didn't intend to hit the ball to put it into play, you can re-tee your ball without penalty. Note that IF YOU SWING AT THE BALL AND WHIFF, IT COUNTS AS A STROKE. If you barely touch the ball or the wind from your whiff blows the ball off the tee, you need to hit your next shot (counting it as your second shot) from where it lies — no re-teeing the ball.

What Do I Do If I Lose My Ball Or Hit It Out Of Bounds?

You read about this situation in Chapter 9 when Barbara hit the provisional ball. Just remember that whether you hit the ball out of bounds or the ball is declared lost, you'll follow the same steps to get your ball back into play.

- **Rule 27-1 Stroke and Distance; Ball Out of Bounds; Ball Not Found Within Five Minutes**

The Rules of Golf allow you to look for your ball for up to five minutes before declaring it "lost." Remember that five minutes seems like an eternity when you are on the golf course, and it is, in terms of pace of play.

Captain Kim Hinshaw (see Chapter 12, *When To Say "Uncle" And Pick Up*) offers this excellent advice about lost balls: "I have a 30-second rule on finding a lost ball. Some balls are just meant to be short-term relationships. A buck or two a ball is not worth taking time away from the other players or getting a rattlesnake bite — rumored to cost up to $75K in medical expenses. Just let it go."

What Do I Do If My Ball Is On The Cart Path?

- **24-2 Immovable Obstruction**

Golf balls occasionally land on the cart path. The cart path is an example of an "immovable obstruction." You get free relief (no penalty) when your ball is on a cart path or other immovable obstruction like a sprinkler head. This also applies when your ball is close enough to an immovable obstruction to affect your stance or your swing if you tried to hit it.

  – In most instances, you pick up the ball and drop it from shoulder height within one club-length of your nearest point of relief (the point where you can take a clear swing at the ball). You cannot drop the ball any closer to the hole, and there is no penalty.

- **24-1 Movable Obstruction**

There are also such things as moveable obstructions. Common moveable obstructions include a rake, a cart path sign, or another player's club, for example. Simply move the obstruction.

If your ball moves during this process, return it to its original spot and continue to play. There is no penalty.

What If I Hit My Ball Into Water?

- **Rule 26-1 Relief from Ball in Water Hazard**

  There are two types of water hazards: yellow-staked hazards and red-staked (lateral) hazards. Yellow-staked hazards are typically the water hazards that you definitely need to hit your ball over in order to complete the hole. Red-staked hazards are typically found alongside the fairway — ideally, you can play the hole without having to hit over them. Depending on which kind of hazard your ball lands in, you have different options.

yellow hazard marker

  In a yellow-staked hazard, you have three options:

  – Play the ball from where it lies without being assessed a penalty stroke. Remember that you cannot ground your club in the hazard.

  – Take a one-stroke penalty. Now imagine a line that passes through both the hole and the spot where your ball entered the hazard (not where your ball ended up). Drop your ball anywhere on that line behind the spot where your ball went into the hazard. You can go back as far as you want, but you can't drop your ball closer to the hole.

– Take a one-stroke penalty, drop a ball and play your next shot from the spot where you previously hit.

Bonus option: Sometimes a par-3 hole with a yellow-staked hazard will offer a drop area close to the green. Take the one-stroke penalty, drop a ball in the drop area and carry on.

red hazard markers

When your ball is in a red-staked hazard and there is no drop area, you have all the options of the yellow-staked hazard plus two more:

– Drop your ball within two club lengths of the spot where it crossed into the hazard, but no closer to the hole.

– Drop your ball within two club lengths of the spot where it crossed into the hazard, only on the opposite side of the hazard. Do not drop your ball any closer to the hole.

NOTE: You can always choose to hit your ball from within the water hazard and, thus, not incur a penalty. (Just make sure your playing partners aren't planning to make you infamous on YouTube.)

How Many Clubs Can I Carry In My Bag?

- **Rule 4-4 Maximum of Fourteen Clubs**

Count the clubs in your bag prior to your round. You may not have more than 14 clubs in your bag without incurring a penalty.

Who Hits First / Who Has "Honors?"

- **Rule 10 Order of Play**

- **Rule 10-2 Stroke Play (Honors). The player with the lowest score hits first on the next hole.**

After the first shot, the player whose ball is farthest away from the hole hits first. This is also the case around the green, regardless of whether or not all the balls are on the green. The rule still stands: whoever is farthest from the hole has honors.

Interestingly, if a competitor plays out of turn, no penalty is incurred and the ball is played as it lies. However, a player in the group can ask the player who hit out of turn to re-hit. This once happened in a **Solheim Cup** match. Annika Sorenstam of the European team chipped the ball into the hole from off the green only to learn she was not the farthest from the cup. The Americans made her re-hit the shot. She did not replicate the chip-in.

Sherry Sentgeorge
Anderson Security

"Your network can really expand when you get involved with a charity fundraising golf tournament. If it's a good cause, it will attract people. And be creative with your networking! Golf makes it easy, because there are so many ways to use it. I was on the planning committee for an all-woman fundraising tournament for a children's hospital. Men wanted to play, but it was an event for women only. It occurred to me to have a caddy auction, which would get men involved even though they weren't playing. I didn't ask permission to do it...I asked forgiveness! It was wildly successful!"

Chapter

15

The Games
We Play

"Most people are paralyzed by fear.
Overcome it and you take charge of your life
and your world."

~ *Mark Victor Hansen*

One of the great things about golf is that the game is flexible, i.e.,
it can be played in various formats. Beginning golfers, for example,
can play in **scramble** format tournaments without the pressure of
having to play their own ball on every shot. Every tournament has a
designated format, but when you are just out playing with friends, it
can be fun to experiment with the basic formats.

When you are invited to play in a charity tournament or business-
related tournament, the format will likely be a **scramble**, **best ball**
or **modified scramble**. The scramble format is very often the
first experience beginning golfers have with charitable and business-
related golf outings.

The scramble format can be wildly exciting because each team player
hits a tee shot on every hole, and then the players decide which ball
is their best shot. When they determine which ball location is best,

each player plays from that spot. The same thing follows for each shot, including the ones on the putting green, until the team holes out. This format encourages fun and camaraderie, and produces birdies and even **eagles**. Many great and lasting friendships have been born during scrambles.

Scramble format tournaments are ideal for groups that include male and female players of all skill levels, because every player has a chance to contribute to the team's success. Perhaps the only thing you do well is putt. That's great! Even if you don't putt well, you can putt first to give your teammates a chance to see the line — and every now and then the hole gets in the way and you are hailed as the hero. Any time you have a chance to participate in a scramble, do it! You'll be glad you did.

Best ball is a popular format that is often confused with the scramble format. Best ball means each player on a team plays her own ball all the way from tee to green. The team's score is the lowest (the best) score of any of the team's players for each hole.

Modified scramble, also called a shamble or Texas scramble, is a combination of the best ball and scramble formats. Each player tees off and the team selects the best shot; then, everyone plays her own ball from that spot the rest of the way to the hole. The team score is the lowest (the best) score made by any of the team's players.

What is a shotgun start? In order for a large group of players to start and finish at the same time, foursomes start off simultaneously on different holes of the golf course. In an earlier time, golf tournaments were often started, literally, with the blast of a shotgun, which could be heard from anywhere on the golf course.

The only potentially confusing thing about a shotgun start is the way you will need to write down your team's score after your first hole. It's likely that your team started on, say, the 7th hole. Out of habit, golfers enter their first hole score in the No. 1 hole column, but in this case it should be entered in the No. 7 column. The final hole for this team would be the 6th hole.

Many charity tournaments have 144 golfers, which necessitates starting two foursomes on each hole. Big tournaments like this often designate those foursomes as "A" and "B." This just means that the "A" group plays the hole first, followed by the "B" group.

If you're playing in a tournament that uses handicaps — golf's way of evening out the differences between players of different skill levels — your total **gross score** is adjusted to a **net score**. In other words, if your gross score is, say, 105, it will be lower after your handicap is factored in and the score adjusted. You could even end up with a score under par!

NOTE: If you don't have an official handicap, no problem! Just inform the tournament organizers or a tournament official that you are a beginning golfer and have not established a handicap yet. They will give you one, and it will be the max!

Mulligans

Aye, a term known by every golfer. In any language, a mulligan is a do-over. A second chance. A freebie. In casual golf, a couple mulligans per round tends to be the accepted norm. However, some unwritten rules apply. As a beginner, take a mulligan or provisional shot when your ball is possibly out of bounds and most likely won't be found. Do not take a mulligan just to try and improve a less than perfect shot. Just play your ball…and go to the driving range for practice. Mulligans are often sold at tournaments to raise additional money for a charity.

Stroke play, also called medal play, is the most basic golf format. It is exactly what the name implies — each player counts all her strokes on each hole and tallies them at the end of the round.

Match play is a format as old as the game itself, and puts the focus on individual holes rather than your overall total score. Each hole is a separate competition. This means, if you have a blow-up hole, it isn't a big deal — it's only one hole.

In match play you win the hole, lose the hole or tie the hole. The scoring is expressed as **all square** (meaning the players are tied),

1-up, 2-up, etc. The match is over when one player is "up" by more holes than there are left to play. A final score of "3 and 2," for example, means one player was up by 3 holes and there were only two holes left to play.

I'm Scrambling!

My friend Chris phoned in a panic! Her biggest client had invited her to play in his foursome in a golf tournament. She had explained to him that she never played except for one time about ten years ago, but he wouldn't take "No" for an answer.

I told her the good news was that he knew she didn't play. There would be no expectations of her. Chris was fun to be around, and her client wanted her on the team because of her personality.

The next week brought another panicked call from Chris. The client had just invited Greg, Chris' coworker, to play in the foursome. "Greg is an amazing golfer, Debbie! His office is full of golf paraphernalia! He talks about golf all the time! I can't do this. I don't want to embarrass myself in front of him!"

We talked it through and she decided she'd play. I asked her to call me afterward to let me know how it went.

She called a few days after the tournament, laughing. She'd had a great time! It was a scramble tournament and she putted first for her team on each hole, to give them the line. One putt was very long and she made it. Her teammates were high-fiving and bragged about her at the dinner that evening. And Greg, she said, was "…terrible! He hit them a far way, but I don't think he EVER hit the fairway! We spent a lot of time looking for his balls in the desert."

Chris ended the call with, "I'm never going to miss one of these again!"

And neither should you!

Allison Suriano
Architect

"I recently participated in a scramble for the American Institute of Architects local chapter. My boss knows I am learning the game. He and I were paired with two 20-something architects who announced on the first tee that they intended to win the tournament as they had in the past. This bummed me out a little since I had to inform them I was a beginner. They said it was no big deal since our scores would be handicapped. We won the tournament! 13-under net score! They used two of my drives, one chip to the green and one putt. What a fun day! The best part was, they commented on how great it was to play with a beginner who appreciated pace of play and knew the rules and etiquette."

Jessica Boutwell
Regional Advisory Consultant
Cole Real Estate Investments

"I couldn't wait to get into the office today so I could talk about the golf tournament I was in on Saturday. I wasn't terrific or anything, but it sure felt good knowing I had absorbed so much information from [the golf clinic]. The biggest surprise came on the green. My teammates called me the 'drainorator' because I kept sinking so many long putts!"

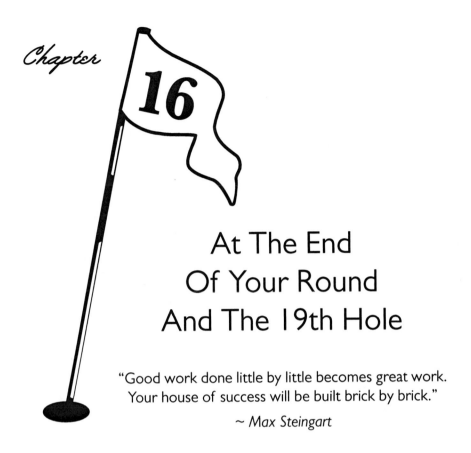

16

At The End
Of Your Round
And The 19th Hole

"Good work done little by little becomes great work.
Your house of success will be built brick by brick."

~ Max Steingart

On your last hole, when everyone has holed their balls, shake your playing partners' hands and thank them for the round. It is customary for gentlemen to remove their caps while doing so. Just like finishing your golf swing, this is the time to set up your follow through. Let a person know you are going to call about something specific, or ask him or her if they have time to meet in the clubhouse (also known as the 19th Hole) for a drink or a bite to eat.

When you return your carts to the staging area, many courses have attendants ready to **clean your clubs** with a wet towel. If tipping is allowed, $2 - $5 per bag is appropriate. If you are the host, cover the tip for your guest(s). Note that this tip is not just for cleaning your clubs — it is for removing your clubs from the car and putting them on a cart, putting them back into your car when you leave, and

 preparing your cart for the round with a scorecard, pencil, cups, towel, etc. Even if you don't have your clubs cleaned, it is still customary to tip the outside staff for all they have done (they pool their tips, like waiters).

Before you leave your cart, definitely double-check to make sure you have all your personal belongings. You'd be amazed how many cell phones, keys and sunglasses get left behind.

If the cart had any issues — bad brakes, lack of power — inform the attendant so they can get those things fixed before the next golfer takes the cart out.

Do a quick inventory of your bag. Count your clubs to make sure they are all there. Are you missing any head covers? Will you need to resupply your bag with tees or balls before your next round? Make a mental note, if necessary.

If you and your guests gather in the 19th hole after your round, take the lead and cover the first round — unless you've been buying beverages on the course. In that case, your playing partners are likely to pick up the tab in the clubhouse.

The clubhouse is the proper place to firm up any business connections that you made during the round. Exchange business cards, swap contact information — whatever you can do to forward the relationship. If appropriate, schedule a phone call or, if possible, a time and place to meet for lunch.

Joyce Friel
President, Peak Performance Consulting

"I started playing with my dad. Anything he did, I wanted to do. My then-boyfriend Joe, now husband (44 years!) played too, and the two of us played with Mom and Dad. Joe and I dated from grade 8 on; we've actually been playing together for 50 years. Today I use golf as a marketing tool — casually, but with a lot of intent. The golf course is a *great* place to do business."

Playing
With Men

"Trousers may be worn by women golfers
on the course, but must be taken off on entering
the clubhouse."

~ *English Golf Club Sign, 1907*

The golf industry was built by catering to the needs of male golfers. That's not an indictment, just a relevant point when considering how women's participation in golf is growing. Women continue to be the largest group coming into the game. Golf course designers are *beginning* to address the fact that men and women are different. *Vive la différence!*

Golf increases your opportunities in the business world. There's no doubt about it. Yet, women DO NOT need golf for networking with other women. Women network successfully with each other over a cup of coffee, a wine tasting, a trunk show, a charity event — the list goes on. Women support and do business with other women.

What golf can give you in more male-oriented business settings is a place on the radar screen. You're included in the conversation. And you have more power in your dealings with men, since golf enables you to cross over easily into one of their favorite "business" environments. This is why women need to learn not only how to play golf, but how to play with men. (And men need to learn how to play with women.)

Playing golf with men will amuse you, delight you, and invigorate you! Know going in that many men believe they should play from the **back tees** because, well, you know, they hit the ball so far. What you'll see, more often than not, is that they *do* hit it far. Far to the left, far to the right — far in every direction but down the middle of the fairway.

You should also know that often, men spend quite a bit of time searching for their golf balls. (There are exceptions to that generalization, of course.) Be patient with them. Maintain your pace of play and demonstrate at least a rudimentary understanding of golf's etiquette and rules — and men will think you are a FABULOUS golf partner. Trust me on this. I've experienced it and heard it from hundreds, if not thousands, of women.

As I mentioned, most men will not play from the Forward Tees. So, if you're playing from the forward set of tees and the men are not, join them on their teeing ground as they hit. You'll not only be able to bird dog where their balls land, helping the pace of play, but you'll create even more opportunities to build camaraderie.

If the teeing ground is not right next to the cart path, then, when it's your turn, ask someone to join you on the tee to help you watch your ball — even if you have great eyes. This can lead to still more relationship building.

Be prepared for your male playing partners to occasionally forget that you have not hit and drive right past your forward tees. It happens. They will be embarrassed and make a joke about it. Laugh with them, at them, for them. Keep a smile on your face.

Men love to help women on the golf course. They'll hunt for your balls, even clean them for you. And they delight in offering advice. Unsolicited swing advice, though, is the worst! If you *want* the input, great. Tell them you are open to suggestions.

If you're not looking for pointers, however, it can quickly become uncomfortable to have someone critiquing your form. Thinking about your swing as you hit is ideal at the driving range – but it can paralyze you when you're on the course. In this case, a great way to curb on-course advice is to tell your playing partners that you're taking lessons (whether or not that's true!) and that your pro has you working on something new. Not only will your impromptu teacher(s) back off, they'll be impressed that you're taking lessons.

Some women tell me they are reluctant to invite a man to play golf for fear it may give the wrong impression. I ask them whether it would be wrong to invite a man to lunch, and they say it would not. Remember that, especially in professional contexts, a round of golf is no different than meeting for lunch. To address their concerns about a man coming on to them, I suggest what I do when I play with men — I bring up my husband (who rocks my world!), my kids, etc. That always makes it clear.

Just a thought: in general, men approach golf with a vision of conquering the game. They focus on the score, distances, winning, betting games, statistics. Most women approach golf in order to create relationships around the game. Be aware of what motivates your playing partners. Be graceful, respectful and attentive. Help them have their best day possible on the golf course, and you'll have friends for life!

Oh — one more thing about playing with men. Ladies, you know how we are. We love to *talk*. Men, not so much. On the golf course, be mindful of this. You know the old saying — if someone asks you what time it is, don't explain how to build a watch.

Jean Ann Morris
Senior Vice President
Wells Fargo Insurance Services

"It was job-related. A majority of the people in my capacity in the insurance industry are men, and insurance meetings always include a golf outing. I wanted to be part of it. The wives go shopping or sightseeing; the men play golf. The first few meetings I traveled to, I discovered that while I was out shopping, the men were playing golf — and talking business. When we all gathered again in the evening I'd ask the men if we were going to discuss *xyz* tomorrow, and they'd say, 'We already talked about that today on the golf course.'"

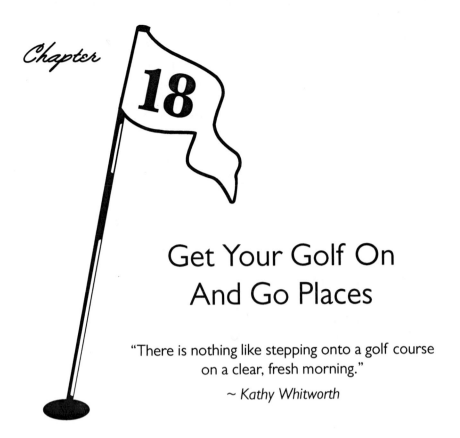

Get Your Golf On
And Go Places

"There is nothing like stepping onto a golf course
on a clear, fresh morning."

~ *Kathy Whitworth*

Golf is a fantastic vehicle for establishing and developing meaningful personal and professional relationships. It opens doors almost effortlessly. Mention that you play golf to almost any new friend, colleague, client or prospect, and you don't just get your foot in the door — you're pulled into the house, so to speak.

The game also provides a wonderful environment for exploring and honing your own skills, strategies and character. You find that it enriches your life in myriad ways. Ask any golfer why she plays and you'll hear her love of the game in her answer. There is just something magical that happens when you hit that little white ball and see it go high and far and right where you envisioned (even if it happens only one time during the outing!).

What Can You Do With Golf?

- **Experience quality time.** You'll experience several hours of undivided attention from clients, business associates, prospects, employees, friends, spouses, relatives, and even strangers.

- **Develop relationships.** Rather than just meeting across a table for lunch, golf enables you to participate, commiserate, and celebrate together. You'll be amazed at how well you can further a relationship without the confinement of business attire and a desk.

- **Learn about others.** Golf does a remarkable job of revealing a person's temperament. How does she react under pressure? What does she like to talk about? Is she respectful? Does she make excuses? Would you consider sending her business or referrals?

- **Challenge yourself.** Most executives are bright and strategy-minded, and golf may be the ultimate game in that respect: it's a constant test of how well you handle the unique circumstances presented by each hole or each shot.

- **Learn a new skill.** Learning never gets old; in fact, learning keeps you interested in yourself and interesting to others. Learning to play golf grows your personal skill set and broadens your professional reach.

- **Network more easily.** Golf is as close as you get to a magical buzzword. If you hear someone talking about their game, someone else's game, or just the game in general, it's an instant opportunity to form a bond — and maybe even get a foot in the door.

- **Connect with nature.** Golf course scenery and surroundings are serene and inviting. Even a well-worn municipal course puts a blue sky over your head and offers a break from the day-to-day grind.

- **Think charitably.** Golf offers myriad opportunities to

give something back to the community. Whether you play, sponsor, or volunteer on a committee, participating in a charity tournament can bring you and your company invaluable community recognition.

- **Reconnect with your family.** Golf is a game that can be enjoyed by young and old alike. It's also something you do together — the perfect excuse for a regular reunion with kids, parents or grandparents!

This last thing you can do with golf, reconnecting with your family, is especially meaningful to me. If you've ever watched an elderly couple dancing at, say, a 60th wedding anniversary, you know how they are carried away by the music, seemingly freed from their aches and pains. For an evening, a few hours, or even just a few moments, they experience a transformation. I see this same thing when I play golf with Maury.

Maury is in his 90s. He doesn't always trust his balance, and shuffles a bit more than he walks. He will grab a handrail if one is handy, or a shoulder, if necessary. But it isn't just out of concern that I keep an eye on Maury at the golf course. He teaches me things.

Maury plays from the forward tees. I watch when he bends over to put a tee in the ground. He is slow and methodical about this, resourceful and efficient too — while he's down there, he always checks for other tees lying on the ground and picks up the keepers. It makes me smile when he does this. It is Maury being a kid. *Transformation.*

I think about a lot of things when I play with Maury. I think about how free of ego and everyday concerns he seems to be. If only all golfers would play the tees appropriate to their skill levels instead of the tees that satisfy their egos. It would help them enjoy the game more, and it would help every foursome behind them. A foursome playing the wrong tees slows everyone else down.

When Maury hits a ball into the rough, he mutters something to himself because he always hopes for a fairway landing, but I know he is not entirely disappointed. I will even say he is not disappointed at all, because Maury loves finding golf balls. He finds his ball, my ball, any ball — even balls the group playing the next fairway over are looking for.

On our 9th and final hole, Maury will carefully line up his putt, but sinking it doesn't really matter. He is on the golf course. That is what matters. Maury, Mother and I always leave the last green arm-in-arm. When we do, I invariably think ahead to the next time when I will bring them to the dance floor and set them free to roll back the years.

There are many reasons we play golf, and the reasons change with the years. If I were asked my number one reason right now, I'm not sure what I'd say, but on the days I play with Maury, I know it with certainty: You live longer.

So, What Are You Waiting For?

Well, all that's left to do now is get your golf on! There are a lot of ways to get in the game and clue others in on the fact that you "know your golf." Here are some to help you get started:

1) Start talking!

    a. Bring up golf in conversations. Keep the excitement alive. Find info to talk about.

        i. Your own experiences; ask others about their experiences

        ii. Listen/watch the Golf Channel and Back9Network — be a sponge! Pick up things via osmosis

        iii. Read the golf section in your local newspaper — might appear just one day a week in the sports pages

        iv. Golf magazines

        v. Online blogs, LinkedIn groups

2) Surround yourself with golf things.

    a. If you work in an office, add a golf book to your credenza, put a putter in the corner, place a photo of you and your friends at the golf course on your desk

    b. Subscribe to a golf magazine

    c. Wear your golf clothes on and off the course

3) And by all means, participate and play!

    a. Find a golf group in your area that offers clinics, leagues and programs for new golfers, especially women — it's so easy to participate in already existing programs. And if it feels safer, grab a friend to join you!

        i. *EWGA* (Executive Women's Golf Association) www.ewga.org

        ii. *Ladies Links Fore Golf* www.LL4G.com

        iii. Local Women's Golf Association in your community

      iv. "Find a Teacher" link on the LPGA T&CP website www.LPGA.com

      v. *Play Golf America* www.playgolfamerica.com

      vi. Get Golf Ready www.GetGolfReady.com

      vii. Call a few nearby golf courses and ask about their clinics and programming for beginning female golfers

      viii. Ask friends for recommendations

b. Take individual golf lessons

c. Visit the driving range

d. Volunteer on a charity golf tournament committee

e. Play in a charity golf tournament

Beth Cohn
Partner, Jaburg Wilk

"I never would have thought of taking up golf if it hadn't been for *Golf for Cause*. I had every excuse under the sun not to want to invest the time, money, etc. into learning to play golf. Yet, I left the breakfast (workshop) with the feeling that this was something I could do and it could benefit me. I've now been playing for three months. I am amazed how many times, in both social and work settings, the subject of golf comes up. Thanks for all of your advice, support and encouragement."

One Last Word Of Advice...

I have met and continue to meet the most fascinating and wonderful people through my engagement with the game of golf. I've developed friendships with people I otherwise never would have met and gained insights that I otherwise never would have realized. One special joy in my life is playing golf with my husband, Jack — not only because it gives us time together, but for the adventures we share seeking out and playing courses wherever we travel.

When technology and busy-ness — computers, commutes, cell phones and deadlines — become too much a part of my daily life, golf takes me away to beautiful surroundings, a change of focus, and uninterrupted time to breathe and daydream and enjoy a round with golf buddies.

I am humbled by my journey with the game and the opportunity it gives me to be in the right place, at the right time, to encourage others, especially women, as they get their first taste of golf or give golf another chance. It is so delightful to watch them grow not only as golfers but as women, developing real confidence that will carry over into other parts of their lives.

And to think I once believed so strongly that golf was boring!

Golf Lingo Glossary

Ace: A hole-in-one. Hitting the ball into the hole in one stroke.

Albatross: A score of three less than par — as you can imagine, a very rare occurrence! You'll also hear "double eagle." It's the same thing as an albatross.

Apron: The shorter grass directly in front of the green.

All square: When the score is tied in match play.

Away: The ball that's farthest away from the hole, as in "you're away." The player farthest away typically hits first.

Back tees: The farthest set of tees from the hole on each hole, also referred to as "the tips."

Ball marker: A coin-sized object, typically round, used to mark the position of a player's ball on the green.

Ball mark: A small indentation on the surface of a green resulting from the impact of a golf ball.

Beach: Slang term for a sand bunker.

Best ball: A format of play typically used in tournaments, in which the team score for each hole is the "best score" of at least one of the players in a foursome.

Birdie: A score of one less than par.

Bite: A ball with lots of backspin is said to "bite," since it stays pretty close to where it landed or even spins back toward the player. Sometimes a player will shout (pray) for a ball to bite if it looks like it's going past the hole. (A humorous way of doing this is to shout, "Grow teeth!")

Bogey: A score of one over par.

Bracket: To take additional clubs — one higher and one lower — than the club you believe you need to hit a certain shot. This means you'll be prepared for a situation different from what you originally expected, so it's generally a good idea.

Bunker: A concave area containing sand or the like, considered a hazard.

Casual water: An accumulation of water on the golf course that is not part of a water hazard. Generally, you encounter casual water after heavy rains. The player is allowed to move the ball without penalty.

Chipping: A low-trajectory, short golf shot typically made from just off the green.

Cup: The four-inch deep, 4.5-inch diameter hole on the green.

Dance floor: Slang term for the green.

Deep: A flagstick or hole that is located toward the back of the green.

Divot: The small chunk of turf that is dislodged when a clubhead strikes the ground as a player hits the ball.

Divot repair tool: A small metal or plastic tool with a prong(s), used to repair ball marks on the green.

Double bogey: A score of two over par. Generally shortened to "a double."

Drained: Slang term for having sunk a putt.

Draw: A golf shot in which the ball gradually moves right to left (for a right-handed golfer).

Drive: The first shot taken at the teeing ground at each hole — even if you don't hit it with a Driver.

Driver: The longest club (and the one with the biggest head), used for tee shots as it's designed to hit the ball the farthest.

Duff: A bad shot.

Duck hook: When a right-handed player strikes the ball such that it curves sharply from right to left and stays low to the ground.

Eagle: A score of two under par.

Etiquette: The rules governing a golfer's behavior.

Executive course: A golf course that is shorter and has a lower par than regular golf courses. Consisting of mostly par-3 holes, it is designed to be played quickly by skilled golfers and to be welcoming for beginner golfers and juniors.

Fade: A golf shot in which the ball gradually moves left to right (for a right-handed golfer). Sometimes called "a cut shot."

Fairway: The center, short-mown portion of a golf hole in between the teeing ground and the green.

Fat: A shot in which the club hits the ground (more so than intended) prior to striking the ball. Sometimes also called "thick" or "chunked."

First tee: Where a round of golf play begins.

Flyer: A ball, usually hit from the rough, that goes much farther than intended.

Fly the green: A shot that goes over the green.

Fore: A warning shouted when the ball is heading toward a person.

Forward tees: The teeing ground located closest to the green.

Fringe: The short grass surrounding the green that is kept slightly longer than the grass on the green.

Get up: A phrase shouted at a ball that looks like it's going to land short of the target. If it looks like it's going to land in a difficult spot (perhaps water or a bunker), you'd say "get over."

Gimme: A putt that is so close to the hole that it's assumed that the player will make it. You can only have a "gimme" in casual, non-tournament play or in match play. An old-fashioned term for this is "in the leather," a reference to the ball being closer to the hole than the length of a putter from the putter's face to the bottom of its grip.

Green Fee: The cost to play a round of golf. (This usually includes the cost of the golf cart rental and practice balls.)

Gross Score: The total number of strokes you take during your round of golf, plus any penalty strokes. Deducting your handicap from your gross score gives your net score. Golf competitions and friendly betting games are often based on your net score.

Grounding: Setting the heel of the golf club on the ground, however briefly.

Handicap: A numerical representation of a golfer's playing ability.

Honors: The right to tee off first, based on having the best score on the last hole or being farthest from the hole.

Hook: When a right-handed player strikes the ball such that it curves sharply from right to left.

Hot: A shot that goes faster or farther than intended.

In Regulation: When a player's ball is on the green in one shot on a par-3 hole; 2 shots on a par 4; or 3 shots on a par 5.

Lie: The position or location of the golf ball while in play.

Lip: The edge of the hole. If your ball hits the lip but doesn't go in the hole, then you have "lipped out."

Loft: The degree or angle of the face of the club.

Match play: A format of golf in which the goal is to win individual holes rather than tallying the total of all of the strokes.

Modified scramble: Also known as a shamble or Texas scramble, a golf format in which the players select the best shot off the tee, move all balls to that spot, and play individual stroke play for the rest of the hole.

Mulligan: In casual play only, a "do-over" shot made to replace a poorly hit shot, taken without counting the stroke toward the score.

Nineteenth (19th) hole: A golf course's restaurant or lounge.

OB: Out of bounds.

Out of bounds: The area outside the course where play is not allowed, most often marked by white stakes.

Pin: The flagstick standing inside the cup on the green. Also known as "the stick."

Pitching: A high-trajectory golf shot made near the green, intended to land softly with a minimum amount of roll.

Playing through: What takes place when one group of golfers passes through another group of slower playing golfers, ending up ahead of the slower group.

Provisional ball: A second ball that is played in the event that the first ball is or may be lost or out of bounds. If the first ball is found and is playable, the provisional ball is picked up. If the first ball isn't playable (if it's lost or out of bounds), the provisional ball is played and penalty strokes apply. Hitting the provisional ball when in doubt about whether a shot went out of bounds often speeds up the pace of play.

Pull cart: A device on wheels that carries a golf bag, used by golfers used by golfers who prefer to walk but don't wish to carry their golf bags.

Punching the greens: Aerating the greens by pulling small plugs (1/4" - 3/4" diameter) or using pokers with small tines that leave the appearance of a pattern of "punched" holes in the turf.

Pure: A well-struck shot, often used as a verb. "She pured her shot!"

Putting: The golf stroke used to roll the ball on the green.

Ranger: The golf course staff member who provides player assistance on the golf course and who is responsible for keeping the overall pace of play.

Ready golf: Players hit when ready in order to speed up or maintain pace of play.

Rough: The long grass bordering the fairway. On some courses, there is a "first cut" of shorter rough and a "second cut" of heavier, longer rough.

Sand bunker: A bunker filled with sand.

Sand trap: Slang for "sand bunker". "Trap" is not defined in the "Rules of Golf."

Sandy: Hitting the ball out of a sand bunker and hitting (usually putting) the ball into the cup on the very next shot.

Scramble: Probably the most popular format for charity golf tournament play. Each player in the foursome hits, then the group selects the best shot. Each player hits from that spot and the process continues until the ball is holed out.

Shank: Be aware, this is a word you should *not* use on the golf course — it's considered bad luck and is therefore a breach of etiquette. However, you should still know what it is: a very poor shot that hits the hosel of the clubhead and "squirts" errantly off to the side. It's sometimes called a "lateral."

Shotgun start: When golfers are sent to every hole so that play begins for everyone at the same time.

Sit: A term shouted at the ball to encourage it to stick very close to where it lands. This is similar to "bite."

Skull: A mishit golf stroke in which contact is made above the equator of the ball, resulting in a line-drive trajectory.

Slice: When a right-handed player strikes the ball such that it curves sharply from left to right.

Smoked: A term describing a well-hit long shot, particularly a drive.

Snowman: A darkly humorous reference to scoring an 8 on a hole.

Solheim Cup: A biennial women's golf tournament in which teams from Europe and the United States compete against each other. It is named after Karsten Solheim (Ping Golf).

Starter: A golf associate who provides golfers at the first tee with any special information they will need during play and maintains the appropriate amount of time between groups of players starting off the first tee

Sticks: When referred to in the plural, "sticks" means golf clubs (as opposed to the flagstick). For example, "I'm buying a new set of sticks this season." A putter is sometimes colloquially called a "flat-stick," due to its lack of loft.

Stroke play: A golf format in which the objective is to finish the game using the fewest total shots.

Sweet spot: The center of the clubface, which will produce the longest shot from a given club.

Tap-in: A very short putt.

Tee box: The area on a golf hole where the ball is first struck, also known as the "teeing ground." Although you hear "tee box" a lot, "teeing ground" or "tee" are the preferred terms.

Tees: Pieces of golf equipment used to raise the ball on the teeing ground for a player's first stroke on the hole. Usually made of wood, plastic or earth-friendly composite material.

Thin: A shot that strikes near the center of the ball, typically causing a low trajectory. Sometimes also called "skinny."

The tips: The farthest teeing ground from the green, usually demarcated by blue, black or gold tee markers. Also called the "championship tees" or the "back tees."

The turn: The halfway point in a round of golf.

Up and down: Chipping or pitching the ball onto the green and putting it into the hole on the very next shot.

Woods: A type of golf club with a round head, usually made out of metal or composite materials. The most common woods include the Driver, 3-wood and 5-wood.

Worm burner: A golf shot (not a putt) in which the ball never rises off the ground.

Yips: The inability to make short putts due to nervousness and lack of a smooth putting stroke.

Zone: When you're playing well, you're said to be "in the zone." Sometimes described as "playing lights out."

About The Author

Debbie Waitkus, Founder and President of Golf for Cause®, is an expert at generating business through golf. Using her own experience as a latecomer to the sport, she helps organizations and individuals, especially women and beginning golfers, use golf as a strategy and tool to achieve goals — to "Turn Golf Into Gold!®"

Debbie was recognized as the 2012 YWCA Sports Leader- Maricopa County, AZ for her commitment to mentoring and motivating women to achieve personal and professional success. Get Your Golf On! brings her passion to an even wider audience.

Debbie is the former president of a $130 million private mortgage banking firm, where she credited golf as one of the keys to her success. She is also a Past-President of Women in the Golf Industry (wigi.info) and a Co-Founder of The National Women's Golf Alliance (nationalwomensgolfalliance.com), with a mission to increase the number of women playing golf, and improve engagement levels of existing women golfers. The group's initiative is called Rolling Out the Green Carpet.™

A sought-after speaker, she also conducts and creates memorable and inspiring workshops, educational golf outings, corporate events and charity tournaments for golfers of all skill levels, even non-golfers.

Learn more about Debbie and Golf for Cause offerings at www.golfforcause.com. She'd love to hear your stories, too! Please post your favorite golf experiences along with comments about Get Your Golf On! to the Get Your Golf On! Facebook page.

Turn Golf Into Gold!®

CPSIA information can be obtained at www.ICGtesting.com
Printed in the USA
LVOW04s2333150813

347929LV00004B/18/P